I0791127

AFTERNOONS WITH GRANDPA

Life lessons from a Tribe Leader

THAMI J. KHALIL

authorHOUSE®

AuthorHouse™ UK
1663 Liberty Drive
Bloomington, IN 47403 USA
www.authorhouse.co.uk
Phone: UK TFN: 0800 0148641 (Toll Free inside the UK)
*   UK Local: (02) 0369 56322 (+44 20 3695 6322 from outside the UK)*

Published by AuthorHouse 09/15/2021

ISBN: 978-1-6655-9280-2 (sc)
ISBN: 978-1-6655-9279-6 (e)

Print information available on the last page.

Any people depicted in stock imagery provided by Getty Images are models, and such images are being used for illustrative purposes only. Certain stock imagery © Getty Images.

This book is printed on acid-free paper.

In Memory of My Father Thami

Grandpa: Haj Jilali

Contents

1

The Art of Useful Inactivity

It was a beautiful spring afternoon. I was on school holiday on the farm at home. The natural setting surrounding the farm was beautiful and inspiring: green wheat, corn, barley fields, and powerful-red poppy and bright-yellow rapeseed fields. Under the active surveillance of a boy, Saleh, hired for the purpose, our cattle had restricted but uninterrupted access to a specific piece of land throughout the entire or part of the day. It was also the season when we enjoyed homemade milk, buttermilk, and butter—all with the taste of the green-flowered fields—prepared by Grandma and my mother.

All this attracted aunts and uncles and their children from the city to spend a spring weekend day on our farm. Sometimes I felt that it was too crowded, too noisy. So, from a distance, sitting in the shade of trees, I watched what was happening. I mainly watched the children running around and getting excited about "finding" eggs, something that my mother did not appreciate too much, but she kept smiling. They loved feeding the horses and donkeys, and laughing and talking to them.

They would ask, "You like that plant, horse? No? And this one?"

They confused mules with horses, or a chicken with a turkey or a goose. They trusted dogs who kept their distance just by fear of being beaten up by my father or my mother. I loved the children's questions to their parents.

"Pa, it is a boy or a girl?"

"Ma, why is this small cow tied by the neck and not with him mom?"

I often mumbled, "Mom, does he go to school?"

I loved watching our animals looking at these children and almost hearing them mockingly say, "Leave us alone! Go away! Stupid children!"

I loved the fresh scents of the season, the silence and the sounds. I heard animals, birds, bees, and the sounds of the trees and dancing fields. I loved thinking that I heard wheat, corn, and barley growing micrometre by micrometre. But what I loved the most were the afternoons with Grandpa. In that season, he was busy cleaning, repairing, sewing, or just deeply, and in long silences, watching nature, sitting in the shade of the tree in front of our house. I had the feeling that he was waiting for something to happen. I often sat next to him. He was busy, while I was reading or just looking around in silence.

On one of these afternoons, Grandpa interrupted the silence and said, "You see, son, all this land around us used to be ours. It was painfully acquired through the hard work of some of our ancestors and easily sold by many of their offspring. This is the consequence of the automatic inheritance process that gives access to property to those who didn't do anything to get it or don't know anything about it."

He continued, "We are fifty settlements in this tribe. Only six settlements are originally from here, and all six are related to each other. All other forty-four settlements came from elsewhere, often pushed by famine and poverty in other areas. Many of them own what we used to have. This is life.

"Our settlement was the largest, with about eighty people. It was a very busy settlement. This busyness was also necessary. You learn this when you live from a business where the working season is much shorter than the nonworking season. Nothing kills the cohesion of a community more than having nothing to do. It undermines the mood, the authority, and the competencies. You learn also that not having something to do does not necessarily mean doing nothing. When you are challenged, you learn to think, to wait. Having periods where there is nothing to do is also something that you have to manage when you lead forty family members and ten permanent resident workers with their families. That is what Ba did with mastery."

Grandpa was very admiring of his father, who he called Ba. After a long silence, he continued. "Ba was an entrepreneur farmer. His was a genius of diversification and anticyclical business creation. Maybe he did this because he had no other choice. Ba had a hundred cows, five hundred sheep, dromedaries, mules, horses, donkeys, dogs … For this he needed enough land, food, water, shepherds, milking force, storage space, and management. So he acquired more and more land, even far from home. He drilled water wells.

He created areas for growing vegetables and planted fruit trees.

"Ba owned tens of pieces of land with several tens of acres each. He was growing crops but also corn, lentils, and onions. Not every piece of land was used every year, as some of it had to rest. Hay was abundant. So having cows, sheep, mules, dromedaries, and donkeys was not to accumulate wealth but to optimize the use of assets and have means for logistics. The food—such as milk, butter, and meat—and activity was for everybody.

"Was this enough? No. There were still three to four months when mules, dromedaries, and donkeys were underused, and there was no activity on the land. So Ba created a new activity: trade in high-quality tissues and garments and also in dry fruits, such as dates, nuts, almonds, and raisins. He purchased all this from Rabat, fifty kilometres away. He used his own caravan as a kind of distribution hub at home. Ba was a good networker. He connected with local notables in the capital, Rabat. His passion for teaching and learning came from there. He created a Quranic school at home and hired teachers for it."

After a short silence, Grandpa added, "When your world is small, you do not need much knowledge to manage it. The world for women was even smaller than for men. We could not predict the change coming for our girls. For reasons of separation, we didn't give girls access to the Quranic school. We had another vision of learning. Reading and writing were skills seldom necessary for rural women, as they were always at home at that time. There was almost nothing to read anyway. We have overlooked the rapid change in that area. It is painful.

"Raising boys was not easy either. They are the future, the reputation, the workforce, and the protection of the settlement. They play around until the age of seven or eight. Some stay at the Quranic school until the age of about sixteen or eighteen. But what to do with those boys who come to an age where they have a huge energy and nothing to do? Set them to work to be busy, to get tired, to grow, to learn, to develop competencies! The entry-level job here is shepherd assistant, son.

"Being a shepherd is not an easy 'being around' job. It is a management job. A good shepherd knows why he is there. Cattle have to grow safely. We cannot trust anyone with our cattle. Being a shepherd requires several important skills. The first one is trustworthiness. We trust them with valuable animals that do not ask for meals or water when they need it; they do not have the choice of the quality of water or meals. Shepherds do this for them. They also create the right environment. Stressed cattle do not take advantage of grazing.

"Shepherds give space and keep control from a distance. They master the art of useful inactivity. They observe cattle movements, know which ones to consider and which ones to ignore. They will tell you that 99 per cent of the movements have no consequences unless we hasten to correct and make them relevant. For the 1 per cent of possibly relevant movements, they can wait until the last minute, and sometimes the last second, before they intervene. They manage lambing and calving the same way and learn to solve difficult cases as they happen. It is energy management.

"This useful inactivity requires knowledge and

observation. It is exactly like with fruits in our garden: We know that there is only one short moment where the shape, colour, taste, and smell are simultaneously the best. It is at that moment and that moment only that fruits are best. This lasts two to three days maximum.

"If you have knowledge, can observe, and can wait, you can have the best quality of fruits. It is the same with all opportunities. The world is full of them, but only a few can be made relevant if we know, observe, wait, and act when it is the right time. No wonder that several of the few big businessmen we have now in Casablanca were first shepherds."

Again, a silence followed before Grandpa added, "Son, you have to spend some time with Saleh. You will learn a lot from him. He is an expert."

I did not react. And then, as if he were reading my mind, he looked at me, smiling, and said, "Son, you may be saying to yourself, *Me? A brilliant student? What can I learn from a semi-illiterate shepherd?* This is the worst advice that your ego can give you, son. Saleh is a master in the art of useful inactivity. This is very difficult to learn. We, and the school, teach you about useful activities. Reading and helping here, for example, are useful activities. Unfortunately, many people fill most of their time with useless activities, like talking for hours about nothing and leaving with nothing.

"Useful inactivity requires the ability to spot opportunities, preparation, and enough patience to wait for the right moment to act. The secret and difficulty are in when to act and when not to. These are fractions of minutes. This is what Saleh masters. If he does not do that, he will be running all the time behind calves and cows, stressing the cattle and being tired. He will be inefficient and will not be the good shepherd he is now. I advise you to go with him in the field and learn from him. It is a useful activity."

After a moment of silence, I replied, "I agree, Ba. I will."

2

The House of Knowledge

It was a nice spring afternoon. The fields were green, red, and yellow, and nature was slowly but surely changing. The weather was very sweet. Grandpa was busy sewing his torn grey "golf" pants under a tree just in front of our house. As I liked watching Grandpa doing things, I came and sat cross-legged on the floor next to him. I think he also liked my company, because at that time he considered me a good learner.

After a long silence, Grandpa said, "Condole him for the loss of his dignity he who cannot mend his clothes, slaughter his sheep, or read his letter. This may seem too much, because nowadays you can pay for all these services. But there are situations where you don't want others to know about your torn clothes or secrets in your letters or to feed you while you have food, and you just have to do something about it. It is about independence and autonomy. Knowledge gives autonomy. There are also situations where you can be a very useful provider of these services to help others. This is the responsibility of this house toward its community."

A long silence followed, probably to give me the time to understand, think, digest, and remember. Then Grandpa invited me to try sewing. "Try it. It is not difficult. It is a repetition of one movement. It is boring. Machines can do it nowadays. But it is a good exercise for your patience. Those who are creative in design and good in sewing are great dressmakers. Your accuracy, concentration, and the quality of sewing needle and thread will make a difference."

Patiently, Grandpa showed me the movement and handed me the needle. I did it almost right the first time.

"Good!" he said. "This is knowledge transfer. We generated in this house knowledge for agriculture and cattle breeding because we are experienced, we experimented, we took risks. We were always early adopters of new seeds, new tools … We share this knowledge and experience. Because we cared about people, we had the best employees. We trained them. They stayed with us, in some cases for generations."

A long silence followed, with deep sighs. I could see in his face that he was sad and angry, two emotions he managed very well. I respected those moments.

Then he continued. "There is no sorrow deeper for me than having young people not willing to absorb the knowledge we share. We do not have much knowledge to share here, and we cannot generate new knowledge because we do not have the opportunity, the means for that. Ba passed away at a critical moment for agriculture in this country: the mechanisation.

"For hundreds of years, our model was built on traditional ways of farming. Our cattle, workers, choice of lands for expansion were based on that. Because many of the heirs were selling the land they inherited from Ba, I felt a responsibility to acquire it. All our investments were poured there. Every time we said that buying back our own land was finished, that we could innovate, somebody else wanted to sell. We could not borrow: it is not lawful, and there were no banks anyway.

"We worked very hard and made sacrifices to be able to buy back the high-value land from our heirs. We have seen during the transactions that we lacked legal knowledge. We learned that there was another power pointing: influence in circles larger than ours. We needed to acquire new knowledge for new battles.

"With your grandma, we have decided to send two of our children to the university in Fez to study Chariâa. The target was that they may become notaries or judges. Your young uncle is studying economy in Casablanca. This is from this time. We kept your father here. He studied Quran. Inspired by some other young people who left the countryside for the city, got a driving license, and learned about car mechanics, he wanted a driving license and is pushing for the mechanisation, at least having a tractor. We just could not afford the transition. We did not allow him to have a driving license. I could not afford for your father to leave the farm or have an accident. We heard about many terrible deadly car accidents at that time. I needed him here. He never understood our selfish decision. He may understand this later."

I asked then, "What is *influence*, Ba?"

"A good question, son. In my experience, you have influence when in few words and actions, you have sustainable and large impact on your environment. Facts are important, but perception plays also an important role in your influence level. A shepherd has a big influence on our decisions when it comes to cattle. But because he is a shepherd, he has a little influence when it comes to community issues, no matter how good or relevant his opinions are.

"Ba was engaged for the community and had a large influence on its constituents. He was the advisor, the conflict manager, the lender for everybody here. When couples had arguments, the wives came here, often with young children. No question was asked before three days, and husbands were *persona non grata* during these days. This rule was accepted. People listened to him and took him as a reference.

"His credibility capital was large, and he managed it very well. He took care of his image. He watched carefully his words and actions. He was conscientious, knowing that others were watching him. He was respected for his knowledge on farming, cattle, and trade; for his connections; and mainly for his people knowledge. He initiated the Quranic school at our home and made it open to all children in the community. Because of this, we earned the title of house of knowledge. It is difficult to have influence without relevant knowledge and acceptance."

"How important is acceptance for knowledge?" I asked.

"Many times," he said, "acceptance of a person as a person makes the acceptance of his knowledge easier. The reverse is not true. We have a good blacksmith in our community. Almost nobody likes him because of his natural rudeness. But because of his high professionalism and the lack of an alternative, people accept his rudeness and use his services. We pray to have acceptance for ourselves and for our products and work on quality. Consistent quality is key to acceptance.

"If the quality of knowledge, for example, is to be seen in something, it is in the quality of decision-making. People of the community watch our decisions and often blindly follow us, up to when to end fasting during Ramadan. We toll the bell at sunset. It is a big responsibility." This was in the time when having a radio was limited.

After a moment of silence, Grandpa added, "I hope you understand what I told you, and if you don't, I hope you can remember something of it. You will understand later."

Grandpa continued sewing in silence. I was watching. When he finished, he asked me, "What do you think about my pants now? You just learned how to mend rips and tears in your clothes, son." Laughing, he added, "You will never walk around with torn clothes. Right?"

"Right," I answered.

I immediately found that I had said *right* too quickly and regretted it. I knew that Grandpa would check on me one day. I had to start practicing mending rips and tears in clothes.

3

My First Day at School

I do not remember when I was left for the first time at the home-based Quranic school for learning. But as far as I can go back in my memory, I have two images:

1. I am on the shoulders of one of the workers crossing the wheat field separating our farm from the home of the scholar.
2. I am sitting on the ground close to the teacher and moving forward and backward, continuously shouting, as were other boys much older than I was.

I learned very quickly that we all had to memorize sentences from the Quran through loud repetition. This way of doing had a reason: the teacher was very old and blind. He needed to hear us. I understood that in that way, he could differentiate the voices and know who was doing well and who was not and call for action.

There were difficult moments for some who were slow to memorize: they were simply beaten on their feet. The mule, as the teacher nicknamed the oldest boy and the slowest to memorize, was often called to help him in beating the soles of the feet of those lacking discipline. He used his cane for that.

There were also celebration moments when one finished memorizing a large part of the Quran or the whole Quran. The last was equivalent to a wedding ceremony, I was told. The "graduated" were qualified to join the club of those reading Quran in ceremonies like circumcisions, weddings, or funerals. Many left the Quranic school early because their ability to work in the fields was greater than their ability to memorize Quran.

The Quranic school was structured. We had breaks at prayer times, along with lunch and snack breaks. We had a day off on Friday. Other boys paid weekly the Wednesday fee, as Wednesday was market day. I didn't have to pay, as the teacher was linked to our house.

It was on a Wednesday early morning, while on the road to the market in the village nine kilometres away, riding on a donkey, that an old guy from the community came up alongside us on a mule and asked my father, "How old is the boy behind you?"

"Seven," answered my father.

"This boy has to go to school, not to the market. I heard from the Quran teacher that he is learning very fast."

"Thank you. Did the school registration start?" asked my father.

"Tomorrow is the first of October. Today is the last day for children's registration. I missed this opportunity for my boy last year, and I regret it. You have to act today."

"Where do I have to go?" asked my father

"You are the house of knowledge, and you do not know? Shame on you! Go to the school in the village. Ask!"

This discussion gave me the sudden feeling that my life was going to change radically and very soon. I had been happy to go with my father to the market in the village, but now I was scared to go there. I didn't know what school in the village looked like. I didn't know anybody who attended school in the village. I didn't want to go there.

The visit to the market that I had waited weeks for became a visit to the school. The dream of spending the twenty cents that Grandpa gave me a day before was evaporating.

After arriving in the village and parking the donkey, my father pulled me to the school. It was a huge building around an open space with an orange tree in the middle and plenty of rooms around. It was larger than our stable. As we seemed lost inside the space, a man came to us.

"What do you need?" he asked my father.

"Sir, I would like to register my son for the school."

"It is too late. Classes are formed. Classes start tomorrow. Try next year," the man said.

I pulled my father's hand and djellaba in a sign that we had to leave the place. But he pulled back. He paused and then said to the man, "This boy knows the tenth of the Quran by heart. He can write and count."

The man laughed. "Are you kidding me? Do you realize what you say? Can you read, write, count yourself?"

"Yes," responded my father. "I know the whole Quran by heart. Let him show you what he can do."

I wished I could not. The man called others. Laughing and shouting, he said, "This man claims that this boy can read, write, count, and knows the tenth of the Quran by heart. He knows more than those who finish the school!"

In no time, I became the curiosity of other people around. The man took my hand and pulled me to a room. The crowd followed, including my father.

The man then addressed my father: "Which tenth of the Quran he knows?"

"The last," replied my father

The man sat on a table, put his hands on my shoulders, and said, "I will start verses. You will finish. Right?"

He randomly selected verses. I finished them all. He took my hand, pulled me to a blackboard, handed me a piece of something white that I learned later was chalk, and asked me to write my name on the blackboard. As I was too small to reach the blackboard, he lifted me up to the level of his shoulders. I wrote my name.

He asked me to write a small verse. I did.

He put me back on my feet and asked me to do some simple mental calculation, which I did. The man lifted me again and kissed both my cheeks.

"He is in! He is my boy now. Bring me today your family record book and a photo of the boy. He needs a blue blouse. He starts tomorrow."

I realized that I had just made my case worse.

My father shook many hands and took mine, and we left the building. We headed to the market. First stop: the photographer. He was there in the open with his strange tool standing on a tripod, with a curtain and bucket with water. After several operations, I got my first ever photos.

We then entered the market with its unlimited number of tents, people, animals, toys, and candies. That's why I'd come in the first place. But now we were heading somewhere else. I discovered very quickly that the blue blouse tent was the destination.

My father bought me a new shirt and a new trouser. Then we rushed to another tent. There was my relief: my grandpa. He had left the house after us.

"Where have you been?" Grandpa asked.

"Your grandson will start school tomorrow," answered my father.

Grandpa, surprised, left a long silence before he said, "Shall we have a lunch? This gentleman does not come to the market every week. Let's take care of him."

During the lunch, I learned that my grandmother on my mother's side had left her second husband and moved with her twelve-year-old boy from our area to the village. My uncle, who I barely knew, would probably attend school too. I learned also that I would probably stay with them for the time being. I didn't know very much about this grandmother. She visited us sometimes. I remembered her for her white skin, blue tattoos on her breast, very blue eyes, and her "Come kiss your grandma."

When my father left for "some business," Grandpa took me on his lap, caressed my head, and said, "If I understood well, you are already a big man. You go to school. You are on your own. I trust you will manage. We will see you every week."

I was thinking that I had not said goodbye to my mother, sisters, and brother. I didn't know when I would see them again. I was not prepared for this. I felt very warm tears flowing down my cheeks.

Grandpa swept my tears with his hand and said, "Don't

cry. A man like you does not cry. You are going to school. You must be happy. Many children of your age would like to have this chance. Don't cry."

Grandpa opened his wallet and gave me another twenty cents. This was exactly the amount that children paid to the Quranic teacher for the week. This remained for me the first time that I was responsible for that money for a week.

My father came back after a while. He took me to my grandmother's house. He discussed things with her and came to me.

"The school is almost at the corner of the street, in the street just behind this one. You cannot miss it. Be there at half past seven. Tomorrow is the first day. I come back on Friday."

My father kissed me and said the words that he would say to me my whole life: "Be a man." Then he left.

I started crying. My grandmother took me on her lap and tried to make things better for me. I was suffocating. The house was small and dark, with one single room, a patio, a very long corridor to the outside, and a terrible silence. I continued crying.

"Go outside, see other children," she said finally. "Play with them."

I was afraid of the outside. It was not my outside.

After some time, my grandmother took me through the corridor to the outside and said, "You see? There are children playing here. You can play with them."

Walls were everywhere—tall, white, threatening. There was no horizon, no dogs, chickens, cows, mules, dromedaries, donkeys. I was alone. There was a tree just before the door. I went to the tree. I felt that, like me, the tree was brought here against its will, so I decided to become its friend. Four hours I was standing against the tree, watching others and thinking to my mother. She had prepared me for visiting the market, asked me to bring something for her from the market, and now I didn't come back.

It became dark. The street was emptying of children. Grandma called me to come inside the house. This was new for me. Just a day before, I was playing with my sister. My house had no inside or outside. All around as far as I could walk away was my home.

I came inside. It was dark and smoky. Grandma was cooking in the open air. I wanted to go to the toilets. There were no toilets. I was in trouble.

Grandma helped me and warned me that next time I would have to go to the "rock." I did not understand what she meant by *rock*. Later I discovered that it was a rock five hundred metres away, outside the village, which was used by all those who did not have a toilet at home.

My uncle came in. We had dinner. The meal had no taste for me, and the bread was different. Grandma noticed that.

"You have bad habits, son," said Grandma. "You have to get used to it."

Soon after, we went to sleep. I laid on the floor with my clothes on close to Grandma. I hated school.

The next day, after a simple uneatable breakfast, I put on my new clothes—my blue blouse. My uncle accompanied me to the school and left me there. He had to go to his own school. The time that a worker could bring me to school was over.

The area before the school was full of boys with blue

blouses, mothers, fathers … In the Quranic school, I was used to being with boys much older than me. I was watching and curious. Then the door of the school opened. Only children were allowed in. Inside, they called names, and we were aligned in six rows.

Then came the man who'd kissed me the day before. He said to us, "There are three classes. Every two rows are one class. Every class has one teacher. You are going to walk with your teacher in rows to your classroom. You do it in silence and with discipline."

Our teacher guided us to one of the classrooms. It was full of strange tables. He asked us to sit down. He then came to me and said, "The director told me that you can write and read. I want you to be in the first row. Come here."

I did, and this made me happy. He called the boys by name and asked us to answer "Present." He then explained to us that there were toilets here and that we could use them during the break. In case of urgency, we could raise our hand and say, "Toilet, sir." This was the best news of the day.

The teacher went to his table. He was busy writing. Everybody was very quiet. I raised my hand.

4

Focus Awake to Learn Asleep

Our community had three weekly markets that could be reached in less than an hour by donkey or mule. These markets were named by the day they took place: Monday, Tuesday, and Wednesday. For our family, Monday market was for groceries, fruit, meat, oil, candles, sugar, thee, and other species. It was situated in the middle of several tribes. Grandpa went to this market mainly for grocery shopping and for meeting other leaders or his friends.

Tuesday was the livestock market and was visited only occasionally by Grandpa or my father. Wednesday market was in the village where I studied. It was nine kilometres away. This was my father's preferred market. He liked visiting administrations, mainly the tribunal and land registration and cadastral affairs, to connect with officials, learn, and sometimes, as Grandpa said, for nothing.

Grandpa visited it for sales of farm products, mainly grain; for paying seasonal farmworkers; and occasionally for some administrative and healthcare matters. Shoeing our donkeys, mules, and horses was also done there.

Wednesday's market often ended an hour or so before

sunset, but Monday's market, much smaller, finished earlier, somewhere in the early afternoon. During my summer holidays, I liked Monday's, as often Grandpa brought back things I liked, such as apricots, watermelon, grapes, mandarin oranges, or even beeswax. Every Monday, at around eleven o'clock, sitting in the shade of trees, I waited outside the farm buildings for his return from the market. I could not miss him: The first man on a mule on the road back from the market was certainly him. Almost invariably, it was around eleven o'clock.

One Monday, after the traditional "welcome back" tea with warm home-baked bread, homemade butter, and honey, I said to Grandpa, "Ba, I noticed that you are always the first to come back from the Monday market. The next one comes at least one hour later. Why?"

He replied, "Son, if you watch carefully, you will see our neighbour coming back about an hour earlier." Smiling, he added, "He is more focused."

Surprised, I asked, "More focused?"

"Yes. Somehow, he is. Focus can be broad and can be narrow. Sometimes I think that our dear neighbour, who is also a cousin, is on the narrow side. He is seldom involved in the community activities or involves others in his activities. He focuses on his agriculture and on his home. That is good. We also do. But I have the feeling that his focus is motivated by a kind of fear of material poverty. He is working hard and driving his family crazy with that. He took his boys out of the Quranic school to help him on the farm. In my opinion, he stays at the market just the time necessary to do some grocery shopping and come back home. He probably comes back earlier because he leaves the market before meat is released by veterinary at about ten o'clock."

"He does not buy meat then. He will hit his wealth-amassing target very quickly," I said, joking.

"Probably," Grandpa agreed. "But wealth is a relative concept, son. Knowledge and education are wealth too. They make you relativise. He may become a large landowner and will have money, yes. But do not let yourself be fooled by that aspect. As far as money is concerned, you will always be wealthier than somebody and poorer than somebody else. Make sure that you develop your intrinsic values. It is worth figuring them out and focusing on developing them, as they will decide what you are really worth in a given environment. If we take you as an example: Writing and reading and maybe counting are all that is relevant for the members of the community. If you can measure land area, you will be of higher value, and this is incidental. Unless you become a civil servant, a medical doctor, a notary, or a judge, all your other knowledge is seldom recognised here.

"What about focusing, Ba?"

"You are focusing when you control your tendency to let your mind wander away from the task at hand, from your target. Do you do your prayers?"

Knowing his tolerance about religion, I answered, "Hmm … Sometimes."

"You know how to do it at least, right?"

"Yes," I said.

"Then you have experienced that if you do not focus during your ablution, you will mess up the count, and you will probably have to start over. Prayers are valid only by valid ablutions. The same may happen during the prayers.

Ablutions and prayers are good focus-strengthening exercises. So, son, practice monitoring your thoughts and focusing. It is important for your effectiveness and also your success. We analphabets, we learn and remember what we learn mainly through focusing. You literates can take notes and reread them, but we cannot. We only rely on our memory. We have to focus to memorise. Good analphabets focus and are very good listeners."

A long silence followed. I think Grandpa did this on purpose to let me absorb and register what he had said. After a while, he continued. "Do not ever assume that an analphabet is not intelligent, son. An analphabet may have limited knowledge, but this does not mean that he is not intelligent. People will often see you from a narrow angle— the angle that is relevant or interesting to them at that moment. They will use that part of you for themselves, and that is what you will be for them. The danger is that you start seeing yourself from that narrow angle too—that your focus becomes limited to their focus. If you do, your neglected broader capacities, maybe who you really are, will die slowly but surely."

"Is that what you called the broad focus?" I asked.

"It is part of it," he agreed, "but not all of it. Broad focus may be difficult to explain, son. An example from our cavalry team may help. When performing, any of our horsemen focuses on mastering his feelings, his horse, his alignment with the team, and performing well. But as the leader of the team, I need to have a broader focus than myself, my horse, and the perfect performance. I have to manage that the team has a common focus. I have to take the team, the public, and the potential impacts of my decisions on them into account, and this not only at the performance moments only but long before that. To be effective, your focus has to be broader than achieving your personal goals. It has to take the people around you, and your environment and its possible changes, into account. This is necessary to have a good positive impact."

He added, "Habits stand in the way of the effectiveness of the focus. You will see more in places where you have never been than in places where you have your habits, and this even if changes happen there. To be better than who you are, choose carefully what you focus on. Focus on what you do, take your environment into account, and welcome changes."

"Right now, I am focusing on my studies," I said.

"That is good. Have also a purpose for that. Have the focus of an analphabet and the broadness of mind of a learned professor. But this is may be for the future. For now, focus on your lessons during the day, and you will rehearse them in your sleep. Focus awake to learn asleep. Take it from me, son."

5

When Lost, Sit Down and Think

My first months at school in the village were far from a happy time. Moving from a wide-open, beautiful, diverse, and secure space to a very narrow, monotonic, and ugly space was a kind of punitive action. I missed everything: my mother who I left saying, "See you this evening" and had not seen since; the fresh bread and its smell; the return of my grandpa from the market; the workers who made me laugh and cared about me; the milk and butter prepared by my grandma; the dogs, chickens, and cows; the silence.

I missed the sweet moments I had at sunrise and sunset, now kept away by the rows of aligned ugly houses. The sun that regulated every activity on the farm was less relevant in the village. The clock took over his power.

Walls, bikes, motorcycles, cars, and unknown people occupied this space, and I had to learn to move in its noisy chaos. I learned that sometimes the hard way. The most impacting event was when I was hit by a car.

Every weekday, I had to cross the main street to go back to my grandma's home. I had the feeling that all the cars in the village were mainly there at that moment. Street lights were sparse and weak. Crossing that main street in the evenings was a nightmare for me—and probably for other children, too, but I was not used to it.

One of the evenings of my first wet season in the village, I left school as usual and ran alone to my grandma's house. It was dark. When I decided to cross the street, I probably didn't appreciate the danger it concealed. When crossing, I was hit by a car. I stood up and ran away without my school bag and without my sandals. A man ran behind me and caught me. I was crying. He tried to calm me and to wipe my tears away. Despite the light rain, a crowd of children and others with indistinguishable faces were all around us in the dark.

"I am Indarouss, the taxi driver," said the man. "I just hit you, my son. I am sorry. Are you OK? Who is your father? Where is your home? Can I bring you there?"

I didn't answer any of his questions just because I had no relevant or useful answer. My whole body was shaking. I was crying. Some children brought me back my school bag and sandals. As I did not answer any questions, and nobody recognized me, the man finally let me go after saying, "Remember, son, I am Indarouss, a taxi driver here. Tell that to your father if he wants to talk to me."

I ran in the dark through the small wood on the way to my grandma's home. Once there, neither my grandma nor my uncle noticed my torn trousers, injured knees, and dirty blouse. I felt abandoned. My grandpa's words "Every time you are hurt, we are also hurt. Think about it when you do things, son" were resonating in my head. "Take care of yourself. Take care of God, he will take care of you." I felt that I had failed him. I needed to see him and to see my mother. I knew that my father would come on Wednesday, but I was not sure about Grandpa. I wanted to go back to my countryside.

The school was not exciting. Being in class with children who had still to be introduced to letters and numbers was boring. This boredom was not diminished by the small books that the teacher gave me for reading almost weekly, nor his taking me to his home to play with his children. These thoughts were strengthened by the growing feeling that I was a burden to my grandma. I felt like she was whispering to me, *Go home!*

I observed my grandma: she was tired of mothering. She had brought up three girls and two boys, most of the time alone, and had done enough. Now she was here in the village because she wanted her last son, aged 18, to go to the regular school, to have a degree and a position. She was not there for me. She loved me, cared for me, but I felt that, somehow, I was a burden that she could not refuse. I felt that the best I could do was be very discreet, "light, very light," with no visible need, no demand. In silence, I decided to leave the school and flee back home. But when and how?

It was a Saturday. For the five remaining days until the next Wednesday, fleeing back home became a kind of obsessive thinking. I had never waited for a day like I did that coming Wednesday. Wednesdays were for me the weekly blessing: I had a school-free afternoon, since my father and sometimes my grandpa were in the village for the weekly market. I was their guest for lunch, and I had a full afternoon with my grandpa when he was there. I received the twenty or forty cents pocket money for the week. But this time was different. I had decided to tell them that I wanted to leave the school and go back home.

When Wednesday finally came, with tears during lunch under a tent in the market, I told my father and grandpa that I wanted to quit school. Reacting to my wish, my father stood up, pulled my hand, took me close to a boy slightly older than me who was washing glasses in the café, and said, "You want to leave school. Fine. This is your future! This is what you want?" Then, addressing the waiter, he said, "Do you need a boy to help you washing the glasses and caring of your fire?"

Surprised, the waiter did not react.

Grandpa, who was calmly watching the scene, asked my father to leave the place. "Go do your shopping. Leave us alone. He is my son, not yours."

Grandpa asked me to come back and sit next to him on the floor. He wiped my tears away with his handkerchief.

"Tell me what is happening, son," he said.

I didn't answer.

"What happened?" he asked again. "I think you are lost in this village. You do not have a reference yet. You feel alone. In fact, everybody who does not have a reference is lost. Your reference is your home, and you want to see it. Right?"

I nodded yes.

"Good. We will fix that. But you have to learn to have new references when needed, son. When lost, we have a tendency to stop thinking. When you are lost, do not run in all directions looking for a reference. Sit down, look around you, and think. Do that also if you are lost in this market. We may be looking for you too. It will be easier to find you when you are sitting somewhere instead of moving around looking for us. Moving without thinking may bring you away from your references or from an opportunity looking for you. So, when lost, sit and think."

I didn't know what to say.

"You want to go home?" he asked.

"Yes," I said.

"Then you are going home with us today. This is also sitting and thinking," said Grandpa.

I was happy, very happy.

When later my father came back to us, Grandpa told him, "Go to the teacher and tell him that the boy is going back home with us for some days."

Some days? I thought. *This is not what I want. I am quitting school!*

My father, who seldom discussed Grandpa's decisions, took me with him to my teacher's home. Fortunately, the teacher was there.

"Master," said my father, "my son misses his mother, and we would like to bring him with us for some days when this is possible."

"This is possible," said the teacher. "Your boy already knows most of the material I am teaching. So far, he is the best in the classes I have. He can miss some days."

I didn't understand what *the best in the classes* meant, but I was happy that this allowed me to have an immediate leave.

My father started a discussion with the teacher on his doorstep. I was pulling his hand, urging him to leave.

When all the shopping was done and my grandmother informed of my departure, we left the market. We travelled back home in a group of several other mule and donkey riders. I was behind my grandpa on his mule. During the nine kilometres travelled, I tried not to be disturbed by the multiple discussions going on in the group. I was dreaming of being back in my bed, the good meals, my siblings, my mother.

When we were almost at home, my mother and grandmother came out to greet us. I was very happy. But when my head became visible to my mother, she immediately asked, "Why are you bringing him back now? Is it holiday time?"

Him was me.

"He does not want to go the school anymore. He wants to be behind the cattle," my father answered.

"He wants to see his mother," Grandpa corrected.

As soon as Grandpa helped me off the mule, I ran to my mother. My mother hugged me. Kissing me, she whispered, "I missed you. The school took you from me. But that is for your own good. Come inside. You will tell me about your life at school and in the village, your life with my mother and brother."

I felt her warm tears on my cheek.

I was at home. I found back my references: the playing space, the animals, the smell of the farm, the warm bread freshly prepared, the evening stories of my mother, the caring of everybody. For the next days, nobody mentioned school, and I thought that the case was closed. But on the next Sunday morning, the signs were not good. The hairdresser was there. My intuition didn't fail me. Later my father came to me and said, "I bring you back to the village this afternoon. Tomorrow you go to school."

"I do not want to go back to school," I told him.

"Then you are going behind the cows tomorrow."

My grandpa reacted. "My son is not going behind the cows," he said. "He is going back to school. I see in him a great man. He has the intelligence of his regretted uncle, my oldest son. He is named after him. He is not lost anymore: he found back his references, and now he goes back to school."

And looking at me, he said, "Right? You see: nothing has changed since the last time you were here. Nothing will change except the nature. And if something will change here, you will do it. For this you need to go to school."

I left the room and went to my mother in the kitchen. I hugged her and told her that I did not want to go back to school. She pushed me away and said, "Why do you think we insist? Because we do not love you? It is for your future. You are lucky to be born in a family that educates and sends their children to school. No one in my family has ever attended any school, except your uncle in the village. They earn their bread with their sweat. Why do you want to stay here? Nothing changes here, nothing. At least at school, you learn something new every day. I do not decide for you, but I agree with the decision that you go back to school."

I was crying.

"Your father told me that you have holidays within two weeks," said Mother. "When you are back then, you will see that these trees will be here, the donkey, mule, cattle will be also here. You will enjoy them more."

She hugged me again.

"I miss you," I told her.

"I miss you too. It is not easy," she said. "Now you have seen me, and you can go back to school. Right?"

I cried in silence. I understood that I had that day no other choice but to go back to the hell of school. I felt that I was still lost. I had nowhere to sit down and think, as Grandpa said. I decided to use the coming two weeks to think about how to get rid of school. Ironically, holidays were popularly named *liberation*.

After the hairdresser, the bath, and the lunch, I was ready to be delivered to my grandmother in the village. My father prepared my grandpa's mule. After I'd kissed everybody goodbye and hugging Grandpa and my mother twice, my father put me on the back of the mule, and we left for the village. After some hundred metres, I remembered that my mother had prepared for me and her mother some bread, eggs, and butter. I told that to my father. My father put me down and asked me to run back home to bring them. When I entered the kitchen, I found my mother weeping and my grandma comforting her.

"Why are you back?" asked my mother

"I forgot the bread, eggs, and butter."

"Oh yes!" she said, wiping away her tears. "Sorry. This is the effect of onions," she added. She gave me a basket, hugged me again, and said, "Go slow back to your father. Do not run. There are eggs in there."

"I want to stay here, *Khti*." (This means sister; I called my mother *sister*, and her nephews called her sister too. She was twenty-four years old.)

"Go before I become angry," she said.

I left. I knew that onions had nothing to do with my mother's tears. I could see that she was also lost. But she would never have time to sit and think.

I hate school, I told myself.

6

Visiting Rules

There was almost nothing to do in the countryside during the holidays except participate in farm activities, listen to the radio, or joke with workers when they were on the farm. I was also limited to rereading, as there was not much to read. I had newspapers that had been used as packing material for products bought in the market; the Quran; a book on Arab medicine from the sixteenth century titled *Kitāb al-Raḥmah fī al-ṭibb wa-al-ḥikmah* intensively used by my father; and some novels with missing pages.

To have some useful busyness, I was interested in joining some of my grandpa's activities, namely going to the markets, attending "board meetings" often taking place at our home, and attending weddings and circumcision ceremonies organized in the community or in neighbouring communities. I liked these activities, as they all took place during the daytime. In contrast to my father, Grandpa did not attend night ceremonies, as music was played there and also to not "embarrass the youth," as he said.

For my grandpa, I had two differentiating characteristics:

1. I was his first and his oldest grandson.
2. I was named after his oldest son. According to Grandpa, that son was a genius. He studied in Fez and had the potential to be a great Islamic scholar and judge but died in his early twenties. According to Grandma, he was poisoned by a jealous family.

This gave me some privileges, but nothing could be taken for granted. I often asked to go with him to the markets or to ceremonies. After many "God willing" answers, he ended up taking me with him to the markets with the condition that I wake up at dawn and help with sales. He had another condition: "When I am in a meeting with people, you sit behind me, you listen, you do not disturb the discussions. You do not kiss hands—not spontaneously and certainly not to people who offer their hands, even if they insist. Just ignore it." It gave me great joy to be with Grandpa in the markets for wheat grain sales, farmworkers' salary payments, and later for his meetings in cafés under tents, sitting in a circle on the floor.

One morning, Grandpa came to me and said, "I go to Haj Kabir today. I may need your help. Would you come with me?"

I did not know the help I could provide that day or the help expected, but I promptly said yes. I was happy that I might have passed the exam of accompanying him and respecting his instructions. He then added, "Go and be presentable. Have clothes with no stain."

While the newness of clothes was important, cleanness was far more important for him than how used the clothes were. "Having new clothes depends on your circumstances;

being presentable depends on you" he used to say. Grandpa was always dressed in immaculate white clothing.

Haj Kabir was the leader of a neighbouring community. He was a respected leader. I had seen him several times at our home. I was excited to go with Grandpa to Haj Kabir's home. I was curious about his environment, his family. My mother was also curious about what they were going to present to us as a meal and urged me to pay attention to the hospitality. As the cook of the family, she knew that leaders are judged by the quality of their hospitality, their bread, their honey and butter, the sophistication of their meals, and even the quality of their plates and glasses.

On the road to Haj Kabir, and after a long silence, my grandpa said, "Son, we are visiting the house of a great man. He still fights, as we do, to keep the community as a community, with members caring for each other. There was a time when we were the system. It is about maintaining and developing community values. Nowadays, we are reduced to being a parallel system next to the administration that is individualizing the society. I do not know what it will be in your time. I hope your generation will continue our services to the community. Anyway, we are visiting Haj Kabir, and there are three visiting rules that you have to observe: limit your field of view as much as you can; eat what is proposed; and, once back home, refrain from reporting on what you have seen, heard, or eaten. Do you understand that, son?"

"Yes, more or less," I replied.

Surprised, he asked, "Which part of what I said is not clear to you?"

Thinking of my mother's request, I answered, "That about eating."

"You do not show any sign, verbal or nonverbal, that can offend your host."

"And if I cannot eat what is proposed?"

"You decline it politely. You do not report on what you have received to anyone."

A boy came from nowhere and took our mule. Haj Kabir came outside to welcome Grandpa. Once inside, I sat just one step behind Grandpa. The visit and the meeting of Grandpa and Haj Kabir went smoothly. I didn't understand most of the discussion, but I observed how they exchanged with each other: they spoke calmly, often approving each other's statement. They listened to each other with sometimes long silences. I think that the long silences were there when they did not agree. The hospitality was excellent.

When we returned, my mother took me into the kitchen and asked, "How was it at Haj Kabir's house?"

"Good."

"Have you been well received?"

"Yes."

"What did you eat?"

"I do not remember."

"You forgot?"

"Yes."

"What a family! You are infected."

I was only observing the three visiting rules that Grandpa told me: limit your field of view as much as you can; eat what is proposed; and refrain from reporting on what you have seen, heard, or eaten.

7

Conceal Your Poverties

It was an August day, a boring day like any other non-weekly market day in the countryside during my summer holidays. Almost nothing happened on those days. Harvest season was over. Seasonal farmworkers were gone, leaving only the two permanent workers. Next to helping with the cattle, my daily busyness was mostly reading or rereading old books or pages of newspapers that were used for packaging, or observing ants for hours.

Grandpa must have noticed my boredom. This is probably what motivated him to appoint me as watchman of the improvised open-air warehouse for wheat bags. I had to keep horses and chickens away and also make sure that no stranger came close to the bags, as theft might happen. Grandpa took me to several large barrels stored separately from the open-air warehouse and said, "These are zakat barrels. If somebody comes here and asks for 'his share' of zakat, please give him from these barrels and from these barrels only."

"How much?" I asked.

"What seems reasonable to you. Use this ten-litre barrel. Do not exceed two full barrels per person."

Grandpa left to join the workers, and I went under the tent to watch the barrels, the warehouse, and the ants. Nothing happened the whole morning. Nobody came. I did have to keep away horses and chickens from time to time, though.

After lunch, Grandpa joined me under the tent. In silence, he sewed something. After a while, a man on a donkey, with dirty and torn clothes, entered the "forbidden zone" and stopped close to the warehouse. I stood up and went to him. He told me that he was selling watermelons.

I loved watermelons. I asked Grandpa if we could buy one. He refused. He explained his refusal saying, "I think that this guy accepts only wheat as payment. Money is not interesting for him. There are two possibilities: We pay him from the bags, but this not what the bags are for. We pay him from the barrels, but we cannot eat something we paid for using zakat."

I was disappointed. I went to the man and told him that we were not interested in his watermelons. Then he said, "What about my share in zakat?"

I turned to Grandpa and asked him what to do. He replied, "You manage."

I went back to the watermelon seller and asked if he had a bag. He handed me one. I went to the zakat barrels, filled the ten-litre barrel, poured its contents of wheat in the bag, and handed it back the seller. But instead of thanking me, he looked at Grandpa and said, "Sir, I am poor, with young children. I came to this great house expecting your kindness. Tell the boy to give me more."

Grandpa looked at me and smiled. I understood that I had to give the watermelon seller more. I was upset that this guy, not happy with my decision, ignored me and addressed Grandpa. Smiling, he hastily got off his donkey, took the bag, and came to the barrels. I half-filled the ten-litre barrel, poured it into his bag, closed the barrel, and walked away.

The man was standing next to the barrel with his bag open. Grandpa told him that was enough. He then closed his bag and asked Grandpa, "Do you need watermelon, sir?"

"No," answered Grandpa.

"It is free for you!"

"I said no," replied Grandpa calmly.

"Thank you, sir."

The man left the area walking behind his donkey. I came back to the tent and sat next to Grandpa. There was a long silence. Then Grandpa said, "I noticed that you were upset. Correct?"

"Yes."

"Why?"

"I was irritated by his attitude of not being satisfied with what he got."

"In your opinion, was he begging, or was he taking chances?"

"Both, I think."

"Son, poverty is ugly. It has several faces. It can be material. But this is relative. We are the rich of many and also the poor of many. But there is a poverty that I find more fundamental: mind poverty. Some rich may be mindly poor and some poor may be mindly rich. It is important to be conscientious of your own poverties and intelligently manage them. Those who show their poverty invite others to despise them.

"Have you seen the clothes of this man? Torn and dirty. He could do something about these two things, but he doesn't. This is mind poverty. But maybe he was showing his poverty on purpose to attract pity. He then sowed his both poverties.

"You too—you have shown a kind of poverty, son. You lost your temper and then probably your ability to manage the situation. So, son, be in charge of yourself. Be aware of your poverties and do something about them, or at least conceal them. Silence, secrecy, and self-control are your best friends for concealing your mind poverty."

He added, "There is one saying that may help for concealing material poverty: 'Eat hay, butter your lips, and dress to impress.' You may not understand all this now, but keep it in mind. The worst poverty is mind poverty. You have to fight it with passion.

"How do I recognize mind poverty?" I asked.

"I do not have a recipe," he said, "but I know it is in cutting corners, in using easy ways in complex situations, in avoiding efforts and work."

Then silence returned. I regretted that I had been upset. I felt it was worse than having torn and dirty clothes. It was a character trait. The watermelon seller must have despised me.

Later in life, I came across what Abraham Lincoln said: "Better to remain silent and be thought a fool than to speak out and remove all doubt." In many situations, we say many things without saying a word.

8

The Sniper's Drama

How I saw Grandpa changed as I grew up and became increasingly aware of how our community members perceived him. I gradually became conscious of the personality he really was through the number of visits he received at home from community members and those outside the community, seeking advice, conflict management, support, or simply courtesy visits. Grandma used to proudly say that "our water is always boiling," referring to being ready to prepare tea anytime for unexpected guests or visitors.

Grandpa had two titles: *Cheikh* and *Moqaddam*. I hesitated for a long time before asking him about these two titles. I finally did on one idle summer afternoon. Grandpa explained that *Cheikh* was mainly for serving the community. The Cheikh is elected by the heads of the families of the community. They first propose two to three candidates and select one. A Cheikh has to be trustworthy and capable of impartially caring for the social needs of every member of the community. He cares for the cohesion and inclusion of the community. Grandpa told me that my great-grandfather was also Cheikh, but this communal position cannot be inherited.

When I asked about *Moqaddam*, he smiled and said, "It is *Moqaddam Rma*. This is different. It is an old story, son. Can you guess what it is about?"

"No. Grandma never calls you by your first name. She always calls you *Moqaddam*. I want to know why."

"Think, son. *Rma*. What does this mean for you?"

"Snipers?"

"Almost. It is about cavalry or what remains from it. It is nowadays a spectacle given by horsemen simulating a cavalry charge. French settlers gave it the name of *Fantasia*, which is, in my opinion, insulting, as in our language this means vanity, arrogance. This was our way of defending our communities and then our country. Rma were warriors."

"What does the Moqaddam do then?"

"He selects the team of voluntary horsemen and leads the team during the performance. Every team member is an owner of his horse. Leading such a team is a challenging responsibility, as it is about reaching perfection while caring about the safety of the team members, of the horses, and also of the public."

"Is the green cloak with yellow inside and the sword we have in the large wooden chest part of the cavalry clothing?" I asked.

"Yes, but for the Moqaddam only."

I understood then why Grandpa was teaching me almost weekly how to catch, tie, bride, groom, and ride a horse. He also often used sayings related to horses:

- Take care of your horse, and he will take care of you.
- Once you are on the horse's back, he assesses if you can lead or he will lead.
- A mule, when asked for a reference, says: The horse is my uncle.

I then asked, "As Moqaddam you had then a real cavalry horse with the nice traditional saddles and bridle. Correct?"

"Absolutely. We had suppliers from Rabat, Fez, and Marrakech."

"Why did you stop?"

"I did not stop, son. It is still here," he said, pointing to his chest. "I quit. In early times, we were investing our time and money for the love of horses and for maintaining the community cavalry tradition. But unfortunately, this muted into a kind of entertainment of officials, side by side with low-taste music and musicians. Instead of being in the lead or involved in the organization of events, as Moqaddam, I started to receive orders disguised as invitations to attend with the team such or such official event to entertain officials. We were losing control of our priorities, of our passion. We felt that the fun and the glory were gone. So, with great grief and sadness, the team was dismantled. I sold the horse, the large tent, most of the carpets, and got rid of everything that could trigger the invitations. We kept some carpets and all the kitchen stuff, as it could be used by the community for ceremonies. All this was part of my identity."

I noticed that Grandpa was still feeling the loss and sorrow. A long silence followed.

He then continued, "Son, when you are riding a horse at full gallop with a loaded musket in your hand, a team around you and the public in front of you, you realize that this is the best that you could do. As Moqaddam, you have to manage yourself, the horse, and the team when you decide to pull the trigger. The best is when the public hears it as one single shot. The right selection of horses, team members, and hand loaders is key, as this decides the quality and the security of people and horses. When I am not sure of the quality and security, we do not participate. These are the most difficult moments. Fortunately, this seldom happened. I must confess that I apprehend the sniper's drama. Do you know what the sniper's drama is?"

Surprised by the question, I replied, "No."

"It is when a sniper works hard and reaches a level where he hits all targets and thinks that he will never miss. The drama begins when he starts to miss and his focus shifts from hitting the target to saving his status or satisfying his ego. He continues shooting but will end up missing all targets and never hitting a single target again. I avoid these situations. One has to learn how to win and where to win. One has also to learn to accept loss and move on. One has to dare to stop when one starts missing targets often. Think about it."

"There are not many snipers around, Grandpa."

"When you talk, you are firing words, son. You can hit the target or miss it. You miss always when you do not have a target. It is when you miss that you hurt yourself. Have a target when you speak, son, and be frugal with your words. Manage your image but avoid being managed by it."

This was one of the most valuable lessons I could have had from Grandpa. Somehow, I was not able to understand it early enough in my life. I had to learn it the hard way.

9

Dress to Impress

As with the doctoral thesis itself, statements added to it have to be defended. In the statements of my first doctoral dissertation, I wrote the following: "Nothing changes but what is seen, and what is seen depends on how it is done." This statement was inspired by the subject of the thesis and also by the simple but essential facts of life. Going from one point to another remains going from one point to another anywhere, anytime. Eating remains eating, getting dressed up remains getting dressed up—but the *how* differs from region to region, period to period. Poor and wealthy alike do the same essential things but do them or experience them differently. The poor and the wealthy in the city are not the same as the poor and the wealthy in the countryside.

My generation lived through a tremendous transition in how Moroccan men in the countryside dressed, moving slowly from Moroccan clothes that were part of a cultural tradition and lifestyle to more Western attire. In the late sixties and early seventies, dress was definitely more conservative in rural areas than it was in cities. Jellaba, a long-hooded robe worn as an outer garment, was more dominating than a coat. While girls in the cities wore miniskirts, it was unthinkable to see a rural girl above her tenth year with an uncovered head. At that time, "modern" clothes were scarce in the countryside.

For some, tyres were shoes, tows were belts, and underwear was almost unheard of. This was almost normal. At the same time, my young uncle who studied and worked in the city wore tailor-made suits and skirts, and always-neat leather or suede shoes. There was a large discrepancy between his clothing style and that of his father, Grandpa, and even my father.

Grandpa's basic clothes at home were three white and two grey pieces. The first white was a *t'chamir*: a single-button-neck long loose robe with long sleeves and a straight collar, crafted from pure cotton. The button was on the right side of the neck. It was also used as a pyjama. The second white cloth was a *farajia*. A farajia is also a long loose robe with long sleeves but with hand-knotted buttons from top to bottom. It is worn over the t'chamir. The third white cloth is *rezza*, a long white turban wound around the head. The grey clothes are *badaiya*, a sleeveless jacket with an inner pocket, and *seroual*, a pant which is like a golf knicker that was also called *seroual golf*.

For outside meetings, celebrations, festivals, and cultural events, Grandpa wore a jellaba or two over the t'chamir and farajia, plus a selham. A *selham*, worn as a cape, is another outer garment that is placed over the jellaba. Often, Grandpa wore striped jellabas and selhams, woven on the family craft alternating wool and silk strips. At home, Grandpa wore a t'chamir and badaiya and, when cold or in the evenings, a regular dark wool jellaba. For shoes, Grandpa wore belghas, heelless slippers made from yellow or white coloured leather. For celebrations, festivals, and cultural events, he wore belghas called Ziouania with a green soft tissue inside.

In summertime, several celebrations, festivals, and cultural events took place in the region. Wedding ceremonies often took place in the evening. They were often attended by the youth and men at the age of my father or slightly older. They were alternately animated by a traditional music group and a group reciting Quran. My father was a member of the latter group.

As I found these ceremonies too noisy and too chaotic, I preferred to stay with Grandpa at home. We were alone with the resident worker. Grandpa attended only some engagements or circumcision ceremonies in the community, as they took place during the day. Every time I saw Grandma and my mother busy preparing farajia and jellaba, I knew that a ceremony was in the neighbourhood. If a selham was added, it was a high-end ceremony or event, probably held outside the community.

Many times, I approached Grandpa at those moments asking, "Can I come with you, Ba?"

I always received *no* as an answer with the argument, "I will not stay long, and it is not fun for you, son. They need you here."

Grandpa often spent only a few hours in the ceremonies and came back before sunset. As soon as he was back, he took off the jellaba and the farajia, put on the badaiya and a work balgha, went outside, and sat on a straw bale waiting for sunset to get the cattle in the stable. I often joined him on the straw bales. I cherished those silent moments, watching the cattle. It was in one of those moments that I had a discussion with Grandpa about ceremonies and clothes.

I asked him, "Ba, I would like to have a suit like that of my uncle Lahcen."

Amused by my demand, he asked, "Why?"

I was not prepared for this. I expected a *Yes, son. Allah willing, when your uncle is here, you go with him to a tailor and have your suit.* Without thinking, I answered, "Because I like it. I never had a suit. I would like to have one for ceremonies, for the upcoming school year."

"Son, with a suit you need a shirt, shoes, socks … this is a heavy investment. Why would I do it?"

"Why does my uncle have more than one suit?" I asked, a bit irritated.

"Hmm," Grandpa mused. "Because he needs them. He is in an environment where this is required. He works in a bank. He now pays for his own suits and what goes with them. When you need suits and are able to pay for them, you will have all the suits you like."

I understood that I had a firm *no* and was disappointed.

Grandpa felt that. He continued, "Your uncle must have followed what we say here: 'Eat straw, apply butter to your lips, and dress to let people wonder who you are.' He works on his image. An image is made of realty and perception. Your uncle cannot dress as the boys from here in the city, and he cannot walk here with his suits.

"The way you dress gives an impression and creates a perception. This is true for everything people see or hear from you—your dress and also your hair, your nails, the tone of your voice. The way you dress has to be age, position, and situation appropriate. You have to become a perception sensor and adapt quickly. Dare to be different but not too different. Just a bit above average to inspire respect, but not too much to create distance.

"But you cannot fool people. In a meeting, people look up to you first for your dress before you sit and then for your knowledge after you sit. It is better to remain silent if you have no relevant value to add to a discussion. So, make sure that you will have both: to dress to impress and to have knowledge to be useful when needed. Knowledge may give you suits, but suits will not make you knowledgeable."

A long silence followed. I was thinking that Grandpa was probably not choosing his dress randomly when attending a meeting or a ceremony. I was thinking that he probably carefully managed appropriateness when choosing what to wear on this or that occasion, and also what to say and when.

Then Grandpa said, "Son, the sun is almost gone. It is time to bring the cattle in. Go and help the shepherd. May Allah bless you with acceptance."

10

Pay Early, Eat Last

Probably referring to working on a rice paddy, a Chinese proverb says, "No one who can rise before dawn 360 days a year fails to make his family rich."

Grandpa had no rice paddy but rose for al Fajr prayer at dawn every single day, and this since he was a teenager. For him, work was a form of worship. At the farm, he grew wheat, barley, corn, lenses, peas, chickpeas, and onions. Even though this kind of farming required limited working days in the year, he worked hard. This had also to do with the cattle he had.

Increasing agricultural output to become rich was not Grandpa's priority, nor an objective. "Live and help others to live," he used to say. To keep the land in the family, he did purchase land, but only from the family heirs. Also, using machines for the sake of increasing productivity was not on his agenda, as generating work for community members was important for him. The transition to a more mechanised agriculture was not an urgent option anyway, as it was costly and required competencies not available in the family.[1] He considered that what was produced at that time was enough. He had also a kind of control, as seeds came mainly from his own production, manure was used as fertilizer, and he and my father worked on the farm.

But a change was in the air. Probably advised by some multinationals and international organisations, government planners may have concluded that the population was rapidly growing and that feeding it would be an issue without increasing agricultural productivity. Supported by the state, access to loans was made easy by the banks for small farmers but exclusively to finance purchasing of new seeds, fertilisers, and pesticides from state organisations and to finance purchasing of tractors, modern combine harvesters, etc. What was not well explained, or probably difficult to understand, or simply ignored by the mostly illiterate farmers is that bank loans were provided at a cost, which was interest on the owed amount.

Grandpa was not sensitive to all these changes. He was sceptical about the loans, their interest, and the new seeds. My father, on the other hand, was enthusiastic and pushy about them. They often argued about their different viewpoints.

After months of negotiations, they finally came to an agreement that the changes, if any, would be done gradually. They agreed first on one piece of land and on one new wheat seed variety to be grown there as a pilot. I still remember the evaluation discussion done after a one-year piloting. While

---

[1] . I learned later that the greatest regret of my father was to not having a driving licence. His father was opposed to it, as he'd heard that many were killed in car accidents or left to the city.

my father was very positive about the much higher quality and quintals per hectare produced, the Grandpa's focus was on other elements.

"I understand your point," he said to my father, "but I am worried about the cost of a quintal per hectare when we use a loan to buy everything needed, combined with the reduction of our added value. We are more spectators than actors. I am worried about this poison, or what you call a weed killer, that we throw in the soil. It kills weeds but also insects and birds.

"I am worried about the social cost too. The work that normally needed ten days is now done in one day. This is true for ploughing, sowing, and harvesting. This new way is exhausting our workers. And what shall they do with the nine free days? If we do not have enough work for them, we will have trouble keeping or finding workers for our regular work in the future.

"And the gleaners? Have you seen gleaners there? They had almost nothing to glean. They already came to me to beg for zakat. And this interest! Why do we need to borrow? We never had a loan with interest. Is that religiously lawful? You must know. You studied for that. This is a booby trap."

A silence followed. My father did not react. He had no property and needed Grandpa's signature for these dedicated loans.

"Having said that, it is your future," Grandpa continued. "You will have to deal with that. I accept to go for a mixed system as long as I am alive. We have a social responsibility and we have to take it."

Grandpa was probably thinking about the two resident workers and their families. They were a kind of an extension of our own family. Grandpa cared about them. Seasonal workers were young guys from the community. My father hired and managed them. They were numerous. During peak moments, feeding them required the combined efforts of my mother, grandmothers, and the wives of resident workers. Their contacts with Grandpa were limited, mainly by respect for his position. They met Grandpa on their payday: the weekly market day in the nearby village.

Joining Grandpa for a weekly market was one of the best moments of my summer holidays—to see different activities than farming and him at his meetings with his friends. For that, I had to wake up at dawn and have a task to do. My tasks were easy: "helping" watching sacks of wheat and barley during the sales or watching our two dromedaries sitting next to each other close to the grain sales area.

I was looking forward to the breakfast under a tent, on the floor, that we had once the sale was finished, often not much later than sunrise. But before breakfast, Grandpa used to go to one of his friends who had a men's clothing store. In fact, the store was a tent with two or three jellabas hanging here and there. The remaining clothes were on a carpet.

After a greetings exchange, we sat on the floor. Grandpa's friend was busy unpacking and organising his shop for the day, and we were waiting. It was too early to do anything else in the market anyway except maybe have breakfast.

One day I lost patience and asked Grandpa, "Ba, why don't we go first for breakfast instead of waiting here for the temporary workers? They will find us or can wait for us."

"Son, we are waiting for those who help us to pay for the breakfast, those who help you to go to school. They will show up soon. We have to wait here. Just be patient."

"And if one of them comes too late?"

"We will wait, and if he is too late, we leave his week's pay with our friend here. But I prefer to meet each one in person. They will not be late. They need the money for their shopping too. I do not want to have anyone from the community telling me 'this or that worker is looking for you.' They already sweated enough for that money. We will not let them sweat looking for us in the market. So, we wait. It is a debt. We have to pay it back as early as possible."

We waited. This "pay early" reminded me of another rule Grandpa had: "eat last." I learned it one hot summer morning at the workers' breakfast time. Their breakfast was served just after sunrise upon their arrival and before our breakfast at home. I came close to the group, who were sitting at the shadow of the house. They were laughing, and the atmosphere was very nice. My father was with them. Grandpa was there, but at a respectable distance.

One worker called out to me, "Come here. Join us for breakfast."

Grandpa heard him and called out, "Come here instead, son."

When I was close to him, he asked me to sit next to him, which I did.

He then said, "We will have breakfast together later. Unless you are going to work with them today …"

"I am not."

"Then eat last. They are in a hurry to go to work. We do not have to distract them. They also appreciate that they eat first. They are celebrated. They have warm bread. They appreciate that they have fresh bread and not leftovers. It is true that they work for a wage. The work will be done, but the wage will be forgotten. They will remember the care. If you care, they care."

Forty years later, I was surprised to see that my mother continued to serve breakfast to the few seasonal workers my parents still had, even if the workers nowadays come at eight and leave at five as in an office. When I made a remark about the usefulness of continuing this tradition, now very demanding and tiring for her, she reacted, irritated, "This house is known by caring for its workers. I will continue doing it as long as I am alive and can. That is also what keeps some of the youth working for us even if we have less work for them."

Remembering the "pay early," I asked her, "When does my father pay them?"

"At the end of their day here They never know if they can come the next day. They do not commit anymore. This gives us a lot of stress. But we do not have much choice. Times have changed."

11

Breaking Stones

On a slow Saturday afternoon in an agreeable early autumn, sitting on a straw bale outside the house building, Grandpa watched from a distance building workers busy breaking and moving stones. Sensing that it was a learning moment, I joined him on the straw bale. After a while, I asked him, "What are these stones for, Ba?"

"The stones were delivered this morning for building a cattle stable. This is your father's project. He is embarking us on unchartered ways of bank loans."

I had heard about this project before. It was an idea of my father to earn his "own money." My father's objective was rearing young cattle—males for slaughter or females for breeding. Stables were new in farming in the community. They were often seen as prestige items. To finance building a cattle stable, my father had accepted a dedicated loan proposal from a bank. Grandpa had to mortgage land to obtain the loan. Using the land he possessed as collateral security to acquire a loan for a building was a difficult decision.

A long silence followed. Grandpa seemed not to be

completely involved in the building project. I had seldom seen him watching from a distance and not directly involved in something affecting our home.

Then Grandpa asked, "How are you doing at school?"

This question surprised me, as we were at the end of three months of summer vacation. It confirmed my feeling that the interests of Grandpa were somewhere other than in this building project. I answered with a quick OK.

After a silence, he said, "What do you mean by *OK*? You stay away from your home for months, you are away from your siblings, you suffer emotional and living privations, and the result is *OK*?"

"I mean, I am doing well. I am often the best of the class."

"I like this better. You have to have clear standards for success and also for failure. An *OK* does not put you on any side: neither success nor failure. If you succeed, have a success that you can build on. If you fail, fail in something that you want to restart, not quit. Look to this project for example. I may be wrong, but for me, the idea seems to come from the bank. The bank will lend us money only if we use it to build a stable and buy young cattle and cattle feed from a cooperative that the bank recommends. This looks like we are executing somebody else's plans. Having said that, your father has my blessing. It is for his and your future."

A long silence and observation of the building workers followed.

"You know, son, these building jobs are new to us here. This house is our first building ever, and it was built in the early fifties by your uncle. We moved into it in the early sixties when he left for the south of the country. He was appointed by the king to be a mayor there. I am still not used to being inside this building."

After a break, Grandpa continued, "I am sceptical about the expertise of these new building workers. I see them often working by feeling. I feel also that they are still learning and experimenting. Most of them are farmworkers and improvise themselves as seasonal builders to earn some more money. It is true that they earn more in building than in farming. It is true that there is not much to do in the autumn."

"Who is their boss?" I asked.

"This guy there who is measuring distances is the boss. He is from the city. They call him master. In the land of blind, the one-eyed man may be king. But he is maybe a real master. Let's wait and see."

I laughed. My grandpa smiled as usual. I didn't remember ever having seen him laughing.

A long silence and observation of the building workers followed before Grandpa added, "Maybe you cannot learn directly from what these boys are doing. They probably do not know themselves what they are doing. But you can learn from their behaviour through observation. Is this something to think about?"

Without thinking, I said, "Yes."

"Observe and tell me."

The words my father told me almost weekly came to me. Laughing, I said, "If I don't work hard enough at school, doing this building work, becoming a waiter or a shepherd, will be my destiny. Right?"

Grandpa smiled and said, "All the jobs you mentioned, son, are not easy as they may seem to be and are far from being an easy alternative for those who drop out of school or fail at their school exams. I am talking about excellence. They require skills that maybe you don't have or you cannot have."

"Strength and toughness?"

"Among others. But this is watching, son, not really observing. I think that growing more as a farmer will help you to develop your observation skills. We have to work on that. Good farmers are good observers. We observe the wind, the colour of the sky, the moon, the soil, the birds, the colour of plants, the behaviours of cattle. Observation is one of the main ways we learn and have information for our decision-making."

To show that I understood his point, I added, "I see young men moving stones and others breaking stones."

"You need to think it through. If you do that, you will see more. Let me share with you two points. First: Be aware of the impression of abundance and manage it. Abundance in my opinion is always temporary. Be cautious about the mirage of time and health abundance. The impression of their abundance in the future may stimulate you to waste what you have of them now. These young boys are not yet aware of their strength and of their health capital. Instead of managing them, they seem to be managed by them.

"There is, for example, a wheelbarrow there. But for some reason, probably their strength and toughness, as you said, they ignore it and keep moving stones one by one. Second: if you want to break a stone, if you know where to hit it and have the patience to hit it long enough, you will eventually break it, even if you are ill-equipped. You never know which blow will break the stone you are hitting. It may be the first blow, but it may be the hundredth. One thing is sure: every blow weakens it more. So it is with projects. Choose which project is worth your energy and time and keep hitting."

Grandpa stood up and went to the building workers. He explained and showed them how to lift the stones without damaging their back and advised them to use the wheelbarrow. He then left to take care of the horses. I kept observing and thinking.

12

Leadership and Fairness

Grandpa was the leader of our community. He was the third generation to hold the position within our family. Despite the fact that he complained sometimes in private about the responsibilities and constraints of the position and the time it cost, he was happy to serve. This involved every member of the family in community activities. He often said that we were chosen not because of the assumed relative wealth and knowledge we have but for the service people expect us to deliver. Grandpa reminded us several times that the function was given to those trusted by the community and that the responsibility lay with every member of the family.

When my father was busy campaigning in local elections, I heard Grandpa once telling him, "Leadership is like expertise: it is more in the recognition of others than in your own statement about yourself. Leaders are entrusted with non-defined missions. In the past, our community entrusted us with the leadership to care for their safety, the security of their property, and the education of their children. In the time that there was no government, no army, this meant that we had to care for the education of the community children, and to protect peace even if we had to go into war for it. The community entrusted us with leadership on the basis of the unspoken condition to be just, fair, and available.

"Today, things have changed. We do not manage the affairs of the community. The administration and civil servants do. Nowadays, people entrust us more with their emotion-related problems, for mediation, conciliation. People love emotions and hate thinking. People expect us to bring thinking into their emotions. This requires the ability to resist the urge to react to uncontrolled emotions or to add our own emotions on to others' emotions.

"When people come to us with a conflict, they expect us to help settle it rather than to judge it. It is there where fair leadership is key. Remember that. But can you still be seen as fair when you have participated in partisan elections? I doubt it."

I was triggered by the fairness aspect of leadership and later asked Grandpa about it. Grandpa answered, "Being fair has first a positive impact on you before having an impact on others. It is one of the best things you can do to yourself. You have to be fair to your body, to your soul. Fairness is a great source of inner peace. If you are unfair to your stomach by overeating, you will not sleep well. It is in fact close to what the prophet said: 'Love for others what you love for yourself.' Justice considers facts. Fairness considers both facts and emotions, in my opinion. You have to be able to evaluate people's perception of your decisions. Fairness is important for our community. It makes conciliation easier."

I learned this from him first-hand and also the hard way. We had at home a shepherd, Salah. I was told that his family had been linked to our family for several generations. He was my age. I was 13 at that time. I was on school vacation at the farm. It was winter. It was raining very hard. The cattle, Salah, and myself were in the cattle stable waiting for the rain to stop. We were joking around.

Then I told Salah, laughing, "Salah, when the rain stops, I will go inside with my books and you will go outside with your beasts."

Salah did not react. But Grandpa who heard me did.

"I do not think that this is correct, son. It is unfair."

I was stunned. I had not noticed that Grandpa was around.

"Salah will go home. He will have a break during your holidays. You take over."

"Why?" I asked.

"Because he needs a break, and there are things you do not learn from books and you need to learn from practice. Salah knows them."

"Such as?" I asked.

"Such as understanding the emotions of those who cannot express them or managing those who cannot understand orders. The beasts, as you call them, will teach you how. They will teach you how important it is to build a trust-based relationship. They will teach you that their feelings drive their behaviour. Beasts will know when you are there to help and when you are there frustrated behind them. They will tell you, son. And if you do not see or understand all this, Salah will explain it to you."

He turned to Salah and asked him to go inside the house and wait for him. When we were alone, he told me, "Son, I find that what you said to Salah is not nice, not fair. You can study because Salah is here. I want you to experience what Salah is doing. You need talent to do it. You have to respect the work of others, to show humility. You will do his work for three days. I hope that you will learn great lessons from it. After that, you will present your excuses to Salah. You may find my decision unfair. But think about it."

I experienced two days of challenges enhanced by the bad weather and loneliness. I had all the time to think about what I had said to Salah, the privilege I had to go to school. On the third day, Salah came back. He proposed to stay with me behind the cattle. We had a lot of fun together.

13

Intelligence, Stupidity, and Learning

Our community had about sixty households. Every household was settled in its own property at a minimum distance of five hundred metres from each other. Only a few adult males were literate, could read Arabic, and could use some of the four basics arithmetic operations. The guy who had the knowledge to measure surfaces of the properties was from a neighbouring community. He could use numbers and was trusted, as he was experienced and very accurate, but he could not read.

For generations, our house had a religious scholar to teach boys from the community Quran, some basics of the religion, prayer times, and arithmetic operations. To the great regret of my grandfather, many boys quit too early and joined the field workers. I heard him once saying to friends visiting him, "In our community, until recently we had a sufficient in-house knowledge and all competencies needed for our daily work. We were learning by doing, and our experience transfer was enough for the young generation. Except for doctors' visits and for official transactions, we seldom needed reading or writing or complex accounting.

Even for our marriages, for many of us, the contract was a prayer and the memory of those who witnessed the wedding ceremonies. Teaching Quran as well as writing agreements is a religious duty. We took this responsibility for the community. All my four of sons know Quran by heart."

He continued, "Unfortunately, few from the community went that far. The change and the rapid complexification of the society is taking us by surprise. We are not prepared to manage it. Our in-house knowledge may be soon insufficient. But every period has its own leaders. If I have a regret, it is of not having our girls in the Quranic school. We have many intelligent girls in our community, but we kept them illiterate. This is nowadays not acceptable."

A long silence followed these remarks. I had the feeling that the guests wanted to avoid a discussion on the subject. So did Grandpa, and, as usual, he communicated this to others, saying, "Please take some more food."

I recognized in what Grandpa said elements from a heated discussion he'd had with my grandmother days earlier about girls' schooling and barriers they faced to basic education. My grandmother had just come back from a long visit to her son in the Marrakech region. My uncle was one of the first Moroccan mayors appointed by a royal decree. As such, he was an official. In those moments of the summer days where there is nothing to do or that can be done because of the high temperature, Grandmother addressed Grandpa: "Moqaddam, I want to talk to you about our granddaughters."

My grandmother addressed always Grandpa using this title instead of his sheikh title in the community.

"I hope good news," he replied.

"Well, not really," she said. "I was in Marrakech. As at our friends' homes in Rabat, I have seen educated, almost sophisticated young girls at our son's home. All these girls say that they learn by themselves from books on cooking, on weaving, on caring for children. They said that they learn from people they do not know, people they never met. Our community girls learn only from us about cooking and carpet weaving, and believe me, it is not much. Some are very clever and learn very quickly. They are hungry for more knowledge, but we cannot feed them. We have nothing to offer to them. I am very angry to see that my daughters, my granddaughters here are illiterate, that their knowledge is limited by our knowledge. This is burning *here, here.*"

While saying these words, my grandmother was tapping on her chest with her fist and wiping her tears with her headscarf. Her emotional reaction about the "impossibility" of giving access to modern education to the girls of our community was in fact an expression of her deep frustration at not being able to do anything about it herself.

Learning was a key word at home, and it was often used with passion. My grandmother used to say that it was not poverty that made people have poor meals at home but ignorance. She heavily blamed the leaders for the absence of learning opportunities and of teachers for it. Grandpa could not agree more with her. The success of our farming activities depended very heavily on his hiring recruitment process and his on-site training and coaching of workers. He was aware that mechanization will disrupt the way of working and that his expertise will not be enough anymore.

Some days later, I was with him under the tent watching the three permanent workers and some other temporary workers busy threshing wheat with horses. He then spontaneously shared with me some of his thoughts on learning and intelligence.

"These boys work hard and seem to be very happy," he said. "I regret that we lose such boys from time to time to the city. Most of those who leave us are serious learners and intelligent, but unfortunately analphabet. I do not know if they make a good choice. The city does not seem to be merciful for analphabets, but despite that, they go there."

I then asked, "Who is an intelligent person to you, Ba?"

"Everybody is intelligent, but to different degrees in different contexts. In my opinion the degree of intelligence can be measured by the speed at which a person analyses and understands his own environment and events and draws conclusions to act or not to act with quality. It is also the speed of learning. Intelligence is a gift. But being serious and a learner is a personal decision. Intelligent people who are learners and serious become great problem-solvers. That is what we need here: quick learners, serious people who can be trusted, empowered. Each environment has its own problems and complexities."

"What is the role of literacy then?" I asked.

"In my opinion and experience as an analphabet," he said, "it is the way to access validated results of the intelligence and work of others. It gives you more ready-to-use knowledge, and more capabilities to solve complex technical, social, and spiritual problems. It enriches your intelligence by the experiences of unknown people. As analphabets, we count only on our own memory as an archive. This is very limiting. An intelligent learner, serious, with a good memory, has everything for success even when illiterate.

"The boys who work permanently with us are intelligent learners and serious in our environment. Unfortunately, because of their illiteracy, they can only enrich their intelligence by the experiences of the elderly, their network, or by their own experiences. I experience that myself. In our community, except for healthcare and to some extent legal aspects, we could manage until now despite our illiteracy. Of course, we can do much better with literacy.

"The environment is important for adding this literacy dimension. It is much easier to be a religious scholar, a notary, a judge when you are intelligent, a learner, and serious, and living in Fez or close to Fez than when living at hundreds of kilometres from it, as we are here. Your both uncles were there. We needed legal people in our family to protect our properties and rights and those of the members of our community. This was triggered by our relations in the city where we have many literate friends.

"You have to have around you people who will challenge you and bring outside what you have inside," he concluded. "It seems that books play the same role. In the whole community here, there are maybe not more than twenty books, Quran included."

I took some reflection time and then asked, "What are stupid people then, Ba?"

"For me, those are problem generators for themselves and for others. They do not learn from their mistakes, sometimes by arrogance. I know many stupid literates." He took a pause and then said, "I am thirsty, son. Go and bring me some water please."

That meant the session had ended.

I went to the clay jar, hidden by workers in a shadowed area to keep the water fresh; poured water in a common cup; and brought it to Grandpa. I was happy with this discussion. Spontaneously, I kissed his head, which was often without a turban when he was under the tent.

14

Milking Dirty Teats

Being born on the only farm in the community with residents and temporary farmworkers does not give an exemption to any family member from working collaboratively to make things happens. Grandpa kept repeating that everybody was needed and that there was no small task and no place for procrastination, as our farming activities were weather-dependent, and convenient time slots were limited.

Keeping livestock or even chickens away from seeds in the ploughing season or from grains in the harvest season was important to Grandpa. I was often assigned this task. I was not happy with it, as I found the task very boring. I was alone, and I found myself continually running in all directions to keep cows, horses, or chickens away from the grains. Once, in summertime, I complained to Grandpa about this task.

He smiled and asked me, "You do not like it, right?"

"Not really."

After a pause, Grandpa added, "Son, I made you responsible for protecting what is the most important component in our activity: seeds and grains. We also want to protect our cattle, horses, and sheep from it. If they eat large amounts of grain, they will become sick or even be poisoned. This is also important. Right?"

"Right. But I do not like running alone the whole day behind our cattle and those of our neighbours who come here."

"What do you like to do then?"

Instead of answering *nothing* or *reading* or *having some help*, as I was thinking, I said, "I would like to be in one of the teams."

"Really?"

"Yes."

"So, if I understand, you want to leave the responsibility you have for what you think is fun?"

"Well. I would like to see how a team works."

"You are still too young[2] for the fieldwork. But you want to do it. We make then a deal: you will join a team, and you will not distract any of its members. You will do the work they do, and you will be paid as the others."

"I do not need to be paid," I replied.

Smiling, he said, "You have to be. You will be accountable. In the Holy Quran, it is said something like: *Do not kill your children for fear of poverty.* You have to ask you father for the exact wording.[3] He knows it. Thinking about you, I say in my words: Do not kill the ambitions of your children through poor thinking. You have your reasons to make that choice. I will let you go with one of

---

[2] I was 15.

[3] "Do not kill your children for fear of poverty—[for] it is We who shall provide sustenance for you as well as for them." *Al-An'am* (*The Cattle*) 6:151.

the teams, and you will be paid as the others. I will wake you up tomorrow morning."

I agreed and said I was happy to get rid of the grain protection task.

In the evening, I informed my mother of what Grandpa and I had discussed. She was worried, but as my father would be around, she agreed. My mother had no saying anyway about what my father or Grandpa decided for me.

The next day, before sunrise, Grandpa woke me up. This was the first challenge—a challenge that I liked when I had to go with him to a market. I joined the teams for breakfast.

Grandpa assigned me to the team for harvesting chickpeas. I received a sickle from the foreman. I knew how to use it. Later, I understood that this assignment was made because harvesting chickpeas can only take place in the morning and before it gets too hot. Harvesting chickpeas early in the day leads to leaving behind fewer kilograms on the ground.

We walked to the field. It was about thirty minutes away. The walk was joyful. There was a lot of fun. Team members were telling jokes or teasing each other. But once in the field, the cutting started at a fast pace. It was like setting fire in a dry wheat field. Nobody was talking. Since chickpeas were close to the ground, cutting them was difficult. Like everybody else, I was working with bare hands. My hands were burning from cutting the chickpeas. But all this did not seem to bother anyone on the team.

I had difficulties keeping up the pace. I expected a break, but there was no break. We were in a race against the sun. A few hours later, we heard the foreman saying,

"Prayers upon our Prophet!" This was the signal that we had to stop cutting.

Everyone put down his sickle and went to the water jars in the tent. Everybody was thirsty, very thirsty. After a small and silent break, sitting on the ground, we left the field and went back home. The walk was silent. I was exhausted. My hands were still burning and my back was hurting. Once at home, we had a meal with milk, fresh baked bread, butter, honey, and tea. When the team left, I went to the living room, which was also my bedroom, and slept.

When I woke up in the afternoon, I went outside the farm buildings and saw Grandpa sitting in the shade of the trees near the house. I went to him and sat next to him. As usual, he did not say a word for a bit, and then he said, "The foreman was very happy with your performance this morning. You did well. He said that you can join the team tomorrow. I was happy with that. It is the last reaping day of chickpeas."

I made no reply.

"How was the team?" he asked. "I hope you learned what you wanted to learn."

"I learned, yes, but I will not join tomorrow. I will watch the grain instead."

Smiling, Grandpa said, "So, you want the glory instead of money?"

"It was difficult, Grandpa. I suffered." While saying this, I was showing my hands to him.

"I understand," he said. Showing me his own hands, he added, "The state of your hands is the first step in making farmer hands like these."

A long silence followed before he said, "Son, I think

there is a lesson to be learned here. The prophet, may peace be upon him, said: 'The paradise is surrounded by hardships and the hell-fire is surrounded by temptations.' In fact, this is true for many things. Look at these cactus fruits just behind us. They have prickly exteriors, with hair-like thorns almost not visible to the inexperienced. You have to get past their prickly exterior to get to the sweet, succulent fruit. Everybody knows that there is a delicious inside behind the prickly exterior. But not everybody knows how to peel them easily. Having the sweet, succulent fruit is all about knowledge and experience. You have to be ambitious in what you want but be aware that it is almost always surrounded by hardships. Be ready to go through them.

"Your objective and motivation for joining the chickpea team were probably not their objectives and motivations. You suffered pain, and they also did. But they were expecting something else that made them accept the suffering more than you did. If you want milk, dirty teats must not prevent you from milking a cow. If you want honey, be prepared for bee stings."

"I like this," I said.

"What do you expect now from going back to grain protection?"

After thinking, I answered, "Your satisfaction, Grandpa."

He smiled. I stood up and kissed his head.

"You are blessed to go to school, son."

"Yes, I know," I said.

15

Honey of Other People's Countries

Every year, I spent the summer school vacation at home on the farm. That year, it was the summer just before my last year of high school. I was attending the most famous high school in Casablanca, and in what was seen at that time as the most prestigious and difficult field: mathematical sciences. I was dreaming about graduating, and that day was close. I had dreams but no real plans for the follow-up.

Since I was a child, instead of using my first name, my father had called me more than often "the crown prosecutor." At that time, the road to that position was through literature studies. Being a crown prosecutor was prestigious to my father, but studying literature was not the right choice according to my middle-school advisors. While I was as good in literature as in science studies, I was pushed into sciences. Those who could not make it to sciences went to economic studies or joined the majority going to literature studies.

At the end of the first year of high school, there was another selection. Those who could not make it to mathematical sciences went to experimental sciences.

Mathematical sciences were considered to be for the elite, the crème de la crème, following the schools' assessors. In the whole Casablanca region, there were only two classes of twenty-five students each in my high school, and a class of female students in a girls' high school.

I was on the path of sciences and engineering or medicine. At that time, there was a limited choice locally: only one faculty of sciences, one faculty of medicine, and three engineering schools—all in Rabat—plus a new civil engineering school that was due to open in Casablanca. While interesting, studying medicine was not an option for me. Studying seven years without an intermediary diploma was out of the question, as my father was warning me at the beginning of each school year that he was happy that I studied, that he was ill, and that he might die that year.

Despite the possible protection of my grandparents, as the oldest of six children, I would have to quit my higher education studies and take over at any moment, probably either as a civil servant or as a teacher. But this did not prevent me from having a dream: aviation!

This idea of aviation came from two influences. The first was that our farm was exactly under the single air corridor in Morocco at that time. This corridor mainly linked the airports of Casablanca and Rabat to Europe. During holidays, I watched several times a day the white trails of what appeared to be smoke left by aircrafts: first north–south and then some hours later south–north. The second element were three men and a city: Antoine de Saint-Exupery, Jean de Mermoz, Henri Guillaumet, and Toulouse. The three men were aviation pioneers, and Toulouse was their workplace. I discovered them through my middle-school French professors of geography and French language, respectively Josette and Claude. They were a French couple from the French cooperation program.

As I was for both a good student, and as I was declared as the best graduating student of all middle schools in the whole province, they invited me to their home for a lunch. It was then that I shared with them my admiration for aviation inspired by the white trails and observation of birds. They gave me a book to read: *Terre des Hommes* (*Wind, Sand, and Stars*).

"Read this book," said Claude. "It is written by de Saint-Exupery, a pioneer aviator. Most of the book takes place in the South of Morocco. He dedicated it to his friend Guillaumet, another pioneer aviator. They were both linked to Toulouse. We think that they both stayed in a villa in this village when de Saint-Exupery flew the Casablanca–Dakar route in 1929 or 1930. We will also find for you the book *Mes Vols* (*My Flights*) by Jean Mermoz, another pioneer aviator. He worked as a pilot on the Casablanca Dakar section in 1926 or something like that. He was also in Toulouse."

I was looking into the book when, smiling, Josette said, "Do you want to be a pioneering aviator here?"

"I do not know yet," I told her. "Eagles are a nightmare for my mother. She fears their attack on her chickens. She often asks me and my siblings to yell and call her if any aerial attacker is in the air, and mainly if it is hovering. So, I observed them. I am curious why chickens do not fly, why ducks fly a bit and only at a limited height and for a short distance, and why an eagle can fly very high and how he can soar and hover. I observe also bees and drones."

"If you want to answer these engineering questions, you have to study aviation," said Claude. "After high school you will have to go to Toulouse, an old and a great university city. We both studied there."

"What kind of aviation courses are offered there?" I asked.

"There is for sure a very good renowned civil aviation school for pilot training in Toulouse. I think you can also study aircraft design and construction and some other aviation-related matters. There are two engineering schools for that there. You have to be good in mathematics and physics. We know you are."

I was just 15, and I had just finished my last year of middle school when this discussion took place. Aviation and Toulouse were great goals to set, but they were also big unknowns and impossible goals. Nevertheless, that afternoon, I left the house of my professors with a book and plenty of food for thought on pioneering, aviation, sciences, and engineering. As I was fundamentally a rural boy, I had just to observe the people and the nature around the farm to spot problems that needed to be solved using science and engineering. Observing and formulating problems was a good busyness, but I felt that I was not tooled to solve them. I had to learn.

The aviation dream kept me highly motivated and committed to study. In the subsequent two years in Casablanca, and despite the very limited access to relevant biographies, I learned to admire pioneers in aviation and problem-solver scientists. I was secretly dreaming of being a pilot or a scientist, but I did not know what, where, or how. My source of guidance was mainly the alumni from the village and show-off sessions during the breaks of some deeply urban and probably also rich students praising their uncles, aunts, and cousins who studied or were studying in prestigious engineering schools in France, mainly Paris.

I could only listen. In my direct environment, I had mainly illiterates. The only one who had a modern education was my youngest uncle, who studied economics and quit in his last high school year to work for a bank in Casablanca. During these show-off sessions, a doom-and-gloom scenario was also mentioned, and with laughs: imagine that you graduate but with grades that are so low you cannot even get a place in the local university. I was not laughing: It was the nightmare scenario. Just a year earlier, we all were students with the highest ranking in our schools. Now some of us had a low class ranking. I had a terrible fear of being one of them.

My anxiety had also a financial justification. Because of my highest rankings and rural origins, I had benefited since my first month in the middle school from a scholarship to be in boarding school. I was accommodated and fed on the school premises. My family had to provide only for my clothing, books, and pocket money. In fact, outside of holiday time, books, and clothes, I was not really putting pressure on the family budget.

But for higher education, the story was different. I could have the dreams I wanted, but if the issue of financing the studies was not solved through a scholarship or family support, "Goodbye calf, cow, pig, chickens," as Jean de La Fontaine said.

I was under no illusion that my family would pay for my higher education, but I needed at least that Grandpa and my father would let me go to university, either locally or abroad. Because of my limited visits to home during the school year, I had only that summer holiday to inform, explain, and maybe also to convince my family of my higher education goals. Before discussing any matter of budget with my father and mother, I needed Grandpa's guidance and wisdom. As usual, I was waiting for the right time to approach him.

We were in the last weeks of September, also the last weeks of the summer holiday. Autumn was here. Despite Ramadan, field burning and soil preparation for the next season were ongoing. I was also helping. I saw an opportunity to discuss the point of higher education with him during a break. Grandpa, the workers, and my father were sitting under the trees. Once the workers and my father went back to the field, I stayed with Grandpa.

I then asked him, "Ba, two of my uncles studied at the University of al-Qarawiyyin, right?"

"Yes. It was a difficult time. Morocco was a French protectorate, as they called it. But in our daily lives, we were under a harsh occupation. No one of the French was here for us. They were here for their own interests. They took the best land, built huge farms, and used people as servants. They stayed here forty-four years. I have never uttered one word of their language."

"Why?"

"Because the language they used was the language of oppression and corruption. All locals who were constantly in contact with them became oppressed, oppressors, or corrupt." Smiling, he added, "Some succeeded in being the three at the same time: oppressed, oppressors, and corrupt."

"French is the language of science and art, Ba," I said.

"I told you. It corrupts. You start to be corrupted, son. I have to admit that since they were here, healthcare, medication, transport, and even the justice system have improved. But they needed them too. Their tax system weakened our collective contribution system. We contribute twice: to the state and to the community."

"Ba, you have been to Mekka by plane four years ago."

"Yes. My seat was close to engines. I still suffer from a headache developed from the engine's noise. Why ask you that?"

"I am interested in airplanes. I would like to study how they work or how to drive them."

"Hmm. Interesting. But why go in the air while there is a lot to do on the ground? Do they teach that nowadays in Casablanca?"

"I do not know. I have to ask. I consider studying abroad if the studies are not in Casablanca. In France, for example. I am sure that there is good training there. My professors told this to me."

Grandpa looked at me as if I were a stranger. He took off his turban, put it next to him, and bowed his head. I understood that I had said something that deeply displeased him, but I did not know what. I remained silent, almost regretting what I had just said.

After a while, he said, "Son, France first took violently our land and resources. We finally sent them back home. Then they took our workers for their farms and factories there. Now you are telling me that France has found a means to drain our talents too? This is dramatic."

"Ba, we do not have enough or the right schools here.

Many students leave for France and come back after graduation as medical doctors, pharmacists, engineers …"

"Many will come back educated, but many will come back corrupted with the French culture too, son. It is like these new modified seeds that we get: high claim, big uncertainty on productivity and quality. Do you see date palm trees here?"

"Yes, Ba."

"Do they give dates as sweet as the palm trees in the south? No. Do you know why? Because they are not in the right environment for that, son. One has to be in the right environment to give the sweet nice fruits. The right environment for you, son, is here. Here you have a legitimacy and the recognition that you will never have anywhere else, ever."

Then followed the usual silence before he continued.

"There is also the fact that we are not used here to seeing our children leaving away from home to places unreachable for us. When your uncles were in Fez in the early forties, I visited them every three months. It took me days because of the lack of transportation and of travel restrictions imposed by the French authorities. When you studied in the village, we visited you every Wednesday. Now that you study in Casablanca, and that is only forty kilometres away, your father visits you every two weeks. You do not see the sorrow of your mother and her tears when she thinks about you. Having you abroad is unthinkable for your mother and father."

Again, a silence …

"You just did with us the field-burning operation. I did that for tens of years. I have never seen a viper leaving its hole during these operations, but I have seen rats fleeing at the first smoke. It is a matter of dignity more than saving their own lives."

"Ba. If it happens I go there, I will go for my studies. I will come back. Look at all these emigrants. They go and come back every year."

"Son, you do not have the same motives or conditions as they do. The saying 'As a medication, tar water of my country is far better than the honey of other people's countries' says it all for me. It is about independence—your independence and that of this country. But anyway. You are still very young. I am too old. I would like not to see you leaving to France in my lifetime. But it is your future: you decide."

"I need your blessing, Ba."

Grandpa put back his turban, looked at me, tapped twice with the palm of his hand on my lap, and said, "Let's go, son. We have to join the workers and your father who prepare the land for the coming season. You do the same for your school year, don't you?"

I joined the field-burning operation with the bitter feeling that I had no clear support, no blessing from Grandpa to go and study in France. There was no need to start any discussion about financing, as even with a scholarship, without Grandpa's blessing, I had to be prepared to drink the tar water of my country if I could not find its honey.

16

The Mentor Passed Away

That year, the transition from summer holidays to the school year was blurry. The first of October, the official start of the school year, was a Wednesday and coincided with the twenty-fifth day of Ramadan. The Eid Al Fitr, the celebration of breaking the fast, was expected to be on the next Monday sixth October or on Tuesday seventh October. This uncertainty was normal, as it was linked to the uncertainty of spotting the new crescent moon on the evening of the twenty-ninth of Ramadan. If the new crescent moon was spotted on the Sunday the twenty-ninth, the Eid would be celebrated on Monday. If the crescent moon was not observed, then the Eid would be celebrated on Tuesday.

I went to school on Wednesday, the first of October, to meet with the professors I would have for the year, to get the list of required books, to choose my bed in the dormitory, and to do some school-related administrative tasks. I went back to the farm on Saturday fourth October and stayed there until Sunday twelfth October. Classes would begin on Monday thirteenth October.

In the past school years, the first weeks always went quite smoothly. I always felt the first month of the school year as a kind of a warming-up time. But this year, it was different. The atmosphere was a bit tense, and professors' and students' discussions were already and mainly about studies after high school. As I did not know what the next year would bring, I focused on the present. The urgency was for me having the required books and necessary clothes on time.

As I was an intern, I was allowed to go beyond the school boundary walls only on the weekends or with a signed request from my tutor. On nineteenth October, I realised that I did not have enough money to buy all the books and clothes I needed. There was no phone, and I could not borrow money from anybody—first, because I did not know from whom, and second, because I followed the saying from Grandpa: "Do not tend your hand to anybody for begging or borrowing: you will get a *no*, bring shame on yourself, or pay back far more than you borrowed. So, manage your needs and desires."

The only option for me was to go back to the farm on Saturday the twenty-fifth of October. Given the transportation issues, to be able to do what I wanted to do, I needed to extend my weekend of twenty-fifth of October by three additional days. For this, I needed an authorisation from the school management. Given the fact that the director knew where I was coming from, that I was never late, that I always respected the rules, and that I was a good student, he granted my request.

On Saturday 25 October, I left the school at about nine o'clock, just after breakfast. After walking kilometres in the city, taking a bus and a taxi, and walking the last two kilometres of dirt road, I reached the farm at about four o'clock. I was happy that it was not raining, as the dirt road turned to mud soup after a rain.

When I was about three hundred metres away, I saw Grandpa sitting outside the building. He also saw me. He stood up, walked towards me, and said loudly, "Why are you here today, son? It there something wrong?"

I could see that he was worried. "No, nothing Ba," I reacted in a calm tone.

Then, because they heard Grandpa talking to me loudly, my brothers, sisters, grandma, mother, and father came outside the house. It was true that since my first school year, I had never come home outside of holidays. I understood that coming back just two weeks after the start of the school year triggered worries.

When we met on my way to the farm, Grandpa warmly hugged me, took my hand, and said, "You must be tired, son. Come inside."

My father joined us. He also expressed his worries. He hugged me and took my bag and my other hand. We walked together to the house.

Once inside, after explaining that I came back just because I needed some more money for books and clothes, I went to the kitchen. The kitchen was the headquarters of Grandma and my mother. At home, I had always the feeling that they were continuously cooking in case a person or group arrive unexpectedly. I received a warm meal. I also received plenty of hugs and questions from my mother. She could not do that in front of Grandpa.

Saturday was for me a weekend day, but for Grandpa

and my father it was just another working day. They were busy outside, as it was the ploughing and sowing season. My money needs were discussed only a day later, on Sunday evening, during dinner. We were only the three of us sitting around the plate.

My father brought it up, smiling. "So, if I understood, you made a budgeting error."

For some reason that I cannot explain, I have always felt uncomfortable talking about money with my father. I replied, "I only have needs, Baba. No wants. I need more books than usual because we are in the year of degree completion. I did not expect that these books would be so expensive. They are newly published books. We have a new programme, we were told."

"Is that all you need?" asked Baba.

"I have a new list from the boarding school. I need a new pyjama, underwear, shoes, and socks. This is compulsory."

"Do you know how much all this costs in total?" asked Baba.

"I do not know. Two hundred Dirhams, I guess."

Laughing, my father said, "This is almost a veal!"

Grandpa was listening. He noticed that I was trying to hide my irritation. He then said, "It will be OK, son." Looking to my father, he asked, "Do we have that cash in house?"

"No," said Baba. "We have paid the daily workers today."

"We are selling grain tomorrow, Monday. On Tuesday, we go to the market to buy a mule. On Tuesday afternoon, we should have all the money he needs," said Grandpa. Looking at me, he added, "How long do you stay, son?"

"I planned to stay until Wednesday, Ba."

"That is good," said Baba. "We are selling carrots and sweet potatoes at Wednesday's market." Looking at me, Baba added, "You can then come with us to the village and from there you go to Casablanca. It is convenient."

"OK. Thank you," I replied.

I was happy with my father's proposal. I was happy that I could stay another Monday at home. Me and my siblings called Monday the red meat day, as we had beef or lamb meat from the market. On the other days, we were vegetarians or had chicken meat when we had unexpected guests. Monday was the day that I waited for grandpa to come back from the market. I waited for the seasonal fruits he brought back and mainly for the tradition of gathering around the tea tray, the warm homemade bread, butter, and honey. This is exactly what happened the next day, on Monday 27 October.

After the tea ceremony, my father, my grandmother, and my siblings left the living room. I stayed. Grandpa lay down on a bench. After a while, I thought it was for a nap. But when I was about to leave the room, he said, "Son, the money you need is ready. Your father will give it to you. You leave tomorrow, Tuesday."

"Thank you, Ba. But Baba said that I can stay until Wednesday. I will go with him to the village, and from there I will go to Casablanca."

"Son, studying is like hunting. It requires passion, patience, accuracy, and ethics. You go into a hunting season well equipped to a place where there is relevant game, with a goal. The hunting season for you this year is open. Your hunting place is not here."

There was a silence. Then he continued.

"You will learn a lot and will forget a lot. Think about what you will take from your production this season as seeds for the next season. Think that you will never have good seeds from a bad production. You will never have a good production from bad seeds or without a good soil, a lot of hard work and sweat. Make always sure that you have good seeds for the next season."

A silence followed. At that moment, we heard the sound of a motorbike.

"Go outside and see who is coming," said Grandpa.

When I was outside, I found that it was my cousin who lived in Casablanca. He was one year older than me. He had tragically lost his mother ten years earlier. My aunt was twenty-seven-years old. He was eight-years-old at the time. My grandmother had continued to grieve the loss of her daughter since her death. She was often bitterly weeping over her loss. Everybody said that crying too much was negatively affecting her eyesight.

Grandma loved this orphan cousin. She hastily came at him with her arms outstretched and hugged him and kissed him for minutes. Grandpa also came out to warmly welcome him. And then there was again a tea ceremony.

Mondays were also the dinners. Monday's dinner was the most important dinner of the whole week as, next to the fact that we had the largest meal, Grandpa and my father discussed Monday's market, the meetings they had, the workers, the equipment, and what should be done in the week to come. But that evening, the focus was on the next day. They planned to go to Tuesday's market to buy a mule, as an additional ploughing team was urgently needed.

They agreed to leave after the dawn prayer, at about five in the morning.

When the dinner was finished and I was given the hand-washing basin, Grandpa looked at my father and said, "Please give the boy the money he needs before you go to bed. He leaves tomorrow morning. We leave earlier. We do not have to wake him up."

"OK, Sidi," replied Baba.

Baba called Ba *Sidi*. Looking at me and at my cousin, Grandpa asked, "The boys are sleeping here?"

"Yes," I replied.

"I will also sleep here," said Grandpa. "It is easier for us tomorrow morning."

This was a very big surprise to me and to my cousin. Grandpa seldom did this. But I was very happy.

We prepared ourselves to go to sleep. When ready, my cousin and I took benches and Grandpa took a larger bench that was often used as a bed.

"Son, do you have matches?"

"Yes, Ba," I answered.

"Then blow out the candle," he advised.

I stood up, went to him, and kissed his head. "Ba, I may not see you tomorrow. Please bless me."

"You are blessed, son, as much as there are stars in the sky."

I went back to my bench. I blew the candle out. In the dark, we heard Ba making his night prayers.

I fell into a deep sleep. But at one moment, I was awakened by a strange noise. It was very dark. I listened carefully. It sounded like a loud snoring. I concentrated for a minute to see if it was coming from inside or outside the room. Then I lit the candle.

It was Grandpa. He was lying next to the door, his face on the ground and his turban next to his head.

I rushed toward him: "Ba, Ba, Ba …"

My cousin came to him too. I was shaking and started yelling and crying. I rushed to my parents' room. I knocked on the door as hard as I could.

My father came out and said, "Calm down. What is going on?"

"Ba, Baba. I do not know what he has. He is on the ground. He does not react."

My father rushed to him, then my mother, my grandmother, and my siblings. Everybody was crying. As my cousin had a motorbike, my father asked him to go to the village to find my oldest uncle, who would bring the doctor, as there was only one in the village.

It was almost dawn. I went outside the house. I sat under the tree where Grandpa used to sit in the afternoons and then moved to the wall facing west, where he sat in the morning, and then moved back to the tree. I was crying. I was praying. I was waiting.

I saw men and women of the community pouring to our house. Then came my oldest uncle in his car, followed by the doctor, in his own car. They went inside. There was a great chaos. Women and children were loudly crying; men were walking silently around as in a market without shops. I was lost. I sat down, I stood up, continuously going from the tree to the wall. Then I saw the doctor leaving. I did not want to know what he found or said. I did not want to think that Grandpa was leaving us.

In the chaos, I heard my name. A worker came to me. "Come inside. Your father is calling you."

I went inside. When I was at the door of the living room, I found that all furniture was removed and that Grandpa was in the middle of the room, lying on his back with his head toward Mecca. He was still snoring, but it was far less loud than earlier.

My father came to me and said, "You go to Casablanca. You will tell all the uncles, aunts, and cousins that Ba had a severe stroke, something in the brain, and that he is between life and death. You have the money?"

"Yes, I have the money for school," I answered, wiping away my tears with my hands.

"Go son. Be strong."

In the taxi I took to Casablanca, I had time to think about all the uncles, aunts, and cousins living there. Grandpa told me once that they mainly were daughters and sons of his brothers who died young from a pandemic in the forties. He brought them up before they left to Casablanca for a job or a marriage. I knew them all—their children and where they lived. When I visited them, I was warmly welcomed, and often I was told, "You are dear to our second father, our protector. When you visit us, it is as if he visits us."

I had also to visit my aunt, the youngest sister of my father. I did not know how to reach my young uncle, the youngest brother of my father. This aunt and uncle were twins.

When I arrived in Casablanca, I was like a zombie. I went to a house, knocked on the door, told the message, saw the deep pain and sorrow, wiped my tears, and left to the next house on my list.

I was back at the farm at around two o'clock in the afternoon. When close to home, I saw a very long cortege of men leaving the house. Almost everybody was on foot. Some were on donkeys or mules. I could hear them repeating two sentences: *lā ʾilāha ʾillā -llāh, moḥammad rasūlu -llāh* ("There is no deity but Allah, Mohammad is the messenger of Allah"). I understood that Grandpa was gone and that they were taking him to the cemetery that was about two kilometres away. I ran to catch up to the cortege.

When I joined, I was pushed to the front of the cortege to join my father, uncles, and cousins. Four men from the community were carrying the coffin on their shoulders. They walked at a fast pace. Once in the cemetery, a prayer was performed, with the coffin placed on the ground before. A dozen Quran readers went to the freshly dug grave. When everything was ready to place Grandpa's body, wrapped in a white linen sheet, in the grave, my father came to me and took my hand. We stood at the edge of the grave. My youngest uncle also took and pressed my hand when they started placing soil in the grave. He was crying.

It was then that I left and walked back home alone. I was not crying. I was not thinking. I was empty. When I was at home, the house was full of women and children. I went and sat under Grandpa's tree.

In the evening, there was a ceremony with about two hundred people present—among them the whole community, many Quran readers, and friends of Grandpa who came from other tribes. I was lost, as this day I buried not only Grandpa but also my mentor, my role model, the man who made me proud to be a peasant when it was an insult in the city.

When all members of the community were gone, my mother called me to have a meal. It was my only meal of the day. I could not swallow. I drank water.

Sitting cross-legged on the patio, my father was loudly crying. My siblings were crying too. Uncles, aunts, cousins, even Grandma were taking turns trying to console him. After a while, he stood up, looked around, came to me, and gave me a long and tight hug.

"Son, we lost our father. We lost our shade tree. Your cousin told us that Ba blessed you before going to sleep yesterday. You were then the last one who spoke to him. That is in itself a blessing. He insisted that you go to school today. Allah had another plan. Ba would not be happy that you will be here tomorrow. You will go to school tomorrow morning. You will have the money you need."

I agreed.

I then looked around to all these tens of members of our large family. I had the strong feeling that many of them would never come back again to this house. I could not explain that feeling, but I had it. Grandpa had left all material things behind, but I had the feeling that many precious immaterial things were gone with him too. I had the feeling that life on the farm and in the community would never be the same again without him. I missed already the afternoons, his long silences, his positive attitude in any situation, and his only two negative words toward others in any situation: *Slaba Hadi*, which means "This is rudeness." I knew that Grandpa would live in me.